housebeautiful

Classic American Decorating

housebeautiful

Classic American Decorating

Text by Rosemary G. Rennicke

A Roundtable Press Book

HEARST BOOKS

A Division of Sterling Publishing Co., Inc., New York

Copyright © 1999 Hearst Communications, Inc.
All rights reserved.

A Roundtable Press Book

Directors: Marsha Melnick, Julie Merberg, Susan E. Meyer
Project Editor: Rachel Carley
Designer: Salsgiver Coveney Associates Inc.
Production Coordinator: John Glenn
Production: Bill Rose

A previous edition of this book has been cataloged by the
Library of Congress.

10 9 8 7 6 5 4 3 2 1

Published by Hearst Books,
A Division of Sterling Publishing Company, Inc.
387 Park Avenue South, New York, N.Y. 10016

House Beautiful and Hearst Books are trademarks owned by
Hearst Magazines Property, Inc., in USA, and Hearst
Communications, Inc., in Canada.

Distributed in Canada by Sterling Publishing
c/o Canadian Manda Group, One Atlantic Avenue, Suite 105
Toronto, Ontario, Canada M6K 3E7

Distributed in Australia by Capricorn Link (Australia) Pty. Ltd.
P.O. Box 704, Windsor, NSW 2756 Australia

Printed in The United Kingdom

ISBN 1-58816-220-6

contents

INTRODUCTION   Like the quintessential melting pot it reflects, classic American decorating embodies a blend of cultural traditions—each distinctly different, yet all part of a broader identity built on imagination, resourcefulness, and the spirit of independence. The intrepid souls who set sail for the New World more than 300 years ago embarked on a venture that ultimately gave birth to a new country whose ideas about government astonished the world. Along with dreams, they brought their own traditions of building and tastes in furnishings. Our multinational heritage, and the rugged individuality needed to begin anew in a wilderness, became the roots of an eclectic style of decorating that has endured and adapted to changing needs. Nothing makes this more evident than the beautiful rooms that fill these pages. We hope that they inspire you as much as they do all of us.

—The Editors

House Beautiful

CHAPTER ONE By definition, a "classic" transcends time and place, trends and tastes. Impervious to shifts in fashion, a classic endures. Whether a well-cut blazer, a sleek sports car, or a superbly composed symphony, it epitomizes excellence by challenging the need for novelty and setting its own standards.

The definition holds true when it comes to American decorating: a classic interior defies geography, architectural style, and the passage of time. The look is equally at home in a southern suburb or midtown Manhattan, in a Federal-period manse or Victorian rowhouse, in a brick ranch or a fieldstone farmstead. And it is as welcoming when rooms are filled with folk art unearthed at a local flea market as it is when high-style antiques and rich fabrics recall the strong European roots of American decorating.

While classic American style may sometimes be difficult to define, it is easy to recognize and appreciate. Consider the seven homes on these pages. Each is decidedly different, but like good manners, all make us feel comfortable immediately. The

classic *style*

rooms have a pleasing sense of proportion and order that appeals to our inner eye. They evoke thoughts of permanence and continuity with carefully crafted furnishings that were meant to last through generations. And they invite our admiration and respect: in an ephemeral, faddish world, some things do pass the test of time.

Classic American style is also easy to achieve by choosing from the diverse range of elements that express its distinctive look. Carved moldings, mullioned windows, and plaster ceiling medallions, for instance, can contribute to architectural character, while glazed walls and stenciled floors begin to provide decorative interest. Furnishings might be as simple as a glass-topped table on a metal stand or as fancy as an Empire sofa with an ornately carved frame and silk upholstery.

And sometimes all it takes is just the right finishing touch to capture a bit of history or express a regional craft heritage — a pretty pottery pitcher, a delft fireplace tile perhaps, or even a tricorn hat propped jauntily atop a polished chest. ⚬━

RIGHT: THE SOFT COLORS OF
SALT-GLAZED STONEWARE
CROCKS, STURDY ESSENTIALS
FROM THE 19TH CENTURY,
BLEND WELL WITH THE
ORIGINAL GREEN PAINT ON A
RUSTIC DOUGH BOX.

ABOVE: A GILT EAGLE
ORNAMENT, A BRASS LANTERN
CLOCK, AND A PEWTER
TANKARD FORM AN UNEXPECTED
ARRANGEMENT ATOP A 1730S
FALL-FRONT DESK.

OPPOSITE: THE CENTRAL ROLE
IN THE FORMAL DINING ROOM
IS PLAYED BY A 1750 ENGLISH
OAK GATELEG TABLE AND
SUPPORTED BY DUTCH,
ORIENTAL, AND AMERICAN
CERAMIC WARES.

period *restoration*

IF HOME IS A TELLING BACKDROP FOR OUR LIVES, then the owners of this 18th-century fieldstone farmhouse in New York State — a set designer and a television producer — have turned their Hudson River Valley retreat into an appropriate theater in which to play out their passions: decorating and collecting. They have dressed the stage with classic architectural elements ranging from plasterwork ceilings to pine-plank flooring and propped it richly with an interesting mix of furnishings.

The resulting interiors are immediately engaging and accessible — as any good performance should be. The 14-room house, which was built in three sections

between 1730 and 1830, was originally home to a well-to-do landowner and served as a speakeasy in the Prohibition era. By the 1980s it lay in near ruins after having been gutted by ambitious owners who never proceeded beyond the demolition stage.

The current owners designed a complete rehabilitation to restore its integrity. Dropped ceilings were ripped out, and for period flavor, antique paneling salvaged from a Colonial-era Connecticut residence was installed in the former kitchen, now the "tavern room." In the living room, hand-carved woodwork, faux-grained by a set painter, recalls the 18th-century fashion for walls with raised paneling.

The desire for comfort keeps the decor relatively relaxed. Such formal pieces as a silk camelback sofa are balanced by homey rag rugs and patchwork quilts. Window treatments are deliberately minimal, consisting of simple valances or swags. A carefully

contrived and controlled color palette creates a sense of harmony with hues designed to flow from room to room: the gray-blue of the entry hall melts into the marine blue of the dining room, which in turn blends into the sage green of the tavern room–kitchen.

Mood, however, was not the only reason for the unobtrusive backgrounds: the real motive was to let the furnishings become the stars of the production. Longtime collectors, the owners selected pieces that appealed to their eye or heart rather than buying strictly by region or period.

This contributes to the personalized feel and prevents the rooms from becoming static museum exhibitions. The assembly of furniture, pewter, paintings, textiles, and ceramic wares comprises pieces from both England and New England and ranges in age from the early 17th to the early 19th century. Fittingly, there are also a number of antiques from the Hudson River Valley, such as a circa-1750 bannister-back side chair and an 1852 coverlet — evidence of the area's preeminence as a furniture-making center from the mid-1600s to the 1800s.

Left and Above: Classic patterns mix effortlessly in this bedroom, where a red coverlet from the Hudson Valley and a blue-and-white 19th-century quilt are layered on the circa-1800 painted pine bed. The patchwork pillow cover displays a traditional pinwheel pattern.

Opposite: The former kitchen has become the "tavern room," where the owners entertain around an 18th-century Pennsylvania cherry table. The imposing comb-back Windsor chair is believed to be from the Wallace Nutting workshop; it joins a set of so-called "Sheraton Windsors" from 1810.

Right: Wool-and-cotton coverlets from the 1800s and patchwork quilts dress a pair of pencil-post beds in cherry, designed by one of the homeowners. The Connecticut corner cupboard, with its original paint, holds English toby jugs.

Federal *elegance*

CHARLESTON WAS A THRIVING SEAPORT AND trade center in the early 19th century, its wealth arising from the rice and indigo that had been cultivated since Colonial days in the lush, loamy soils of South Carolina. And like many another of the city's successful merchants at the time, Benjamin Philips displayed his good fortune, and good taste, by building a gracious residence in the Federal style. Simple yet elegant, his three-and-one-half-story townhouse, erected in 1818, was appointed with the architectural features then in fashion, such as Greek key moldings, fluted pilasters, and archways.

BELOW: HAND-PAINTED IN HONG KONG, THE DINING-ROOM WALLPAPER IS AMERICAN IN THEME YET VAGUELY ASIAN IN STYLE, IN KEEPING WITH THE FEDERAL-ERA TASTE FOR ALL THINGS ORIENTAL.

OPPOSITE: SUBDUED PAINT COLORS AND ELEGANTLY LIGHT HEPPLEWHITE FURNITURE MADE OF MAHOGANY DISTINGUISH THE SAME ROOM AND PERMIT THE WALLPAPER TO BE THE DOMINANT FEATURE.

Some 150 years later, however, the house was chopped into apartments. It took an exhaustive renovation, grounded in on-site historical evidence and aided by the Historic Charleston Foundation, to return the interiors to their former dignity, complete with Federal furnishings.

The owners wanted a "legitimate, authentic restoration," says the designer, Cozy Pelzer, that was also pleasurable to live and entertain in. They began with the architectural elements. Antique heart-pine flooring filled in where original boards had been destroyed, and painstaking hand cleaning of the woodwork lifted layers of paint so thick they had obscured delicate moldings. Even the fireplace mantel in the library was replicated with early 19th-century panels of black cypress hand planed and carved with Neoclassical designs.

It was in the early 1800s that American interiors first became light and airy; muted paint colors and wallpapers with delicate patterns were the height of fashion. In keeping with that taste, the Philips house glows softly with celadon green, citrus yellow, and biscuit-beige paints, and the two main rooms boast exquisite wallpapers that reflect important decorative traditions of the day. The

OPPOSITE: A MOLDED ARCH, A CLASSICAL ELEMENT COMMON TO FEDERAL ARCHITECTURE, FRAMES A COUNTRY SHIELD-BACK SETTEE, CIRCA 1800. THE 1795 PAINTING IS BY A CONNECTICUT PORTRAITIST TRAINED IN ENGLAND.

ABOVE: LIBRARY BOOKSHELVES ECHO THE ELLIPSE AND PILASTER DETAILS OF THE FIREPLACE. DAMASK-LOOK UPHOLSTERY IN GLAZED RED COTTON IS PRACTICAL, YET ORNATE ENOUGH FOR THE FEDERAL STYLE.

drawing-room paper adapts a Chinese design, recalling the Oriental wallpapers imported to America in the early 19th century, when trade with, and interest in, eastern Asia was increasing. The romantic harbor scene in the dining room was inspired by a circa-1830 mural in a New York house by William Price, an itinerant ornamental painter. That this paper's Americana theme was rendered in a vaguely Asian style only accentuates its charm.

Although not necessarily characteristic of the period, some of the original woodwork, such as the dado and trim in the drawing room, remains unpainted. The subdued golden-gray undertones of the aged cypress wood blend perfectly with the wallpaper's color scheme, and the "unfinished" look provides a welcome balance to the elaborate Oriental motifs.

Sophisticated furniture also underscores the authenticity of the interiors. Furnishings in the Federal era were very refined, designed with pleasing proportions and restrained forms based on Classical art and constructed of exotic woods. Many pieces in the Philips House are in

THE INTRICATE WOODWORK IN THE DRAWING ROOM — INCLUDING AN ARCHED CORNICE MOLDING, BEADED WINDOW TRIM WITH CARVED ROSETTES THAT PRECISELY REPRODUCE THE ORIGINALS, AND A GREEK-KEY CHAIR RAIL — LOOKS ELEGANT EVEN WHEN LEFT UNPAINTED. SILK DAMASK FABRICS PICK UP THE COLORS IN BOTH THE HAND-PAINTED CHINESE-PATTERN WALLPAPER AND THE PATINA OF THE ORIGINAL CYPRESS PANELS.

the Hepplewhite style, their carving and curvilinear silhouettes recalling the designs that English furniture-maker George Hepplewhite popularized in his *Cabinet-Maker and Upholsterer's Guide* of 1788. The English Hepplewhite mahogany dining table, for instance, is joined by shield-back chairs that feature characteristically fine swag motifs.

Another hallmark of the Federal style is the coordination of fabrics: typically silk or satin for the "best" rooms and chintz elsewhere. For the drawing room upholstery and window treatments, Pelzer chose a silk damask with an apricot floral pattern on a silver-gray ground; the drapery linings and pillows are in the same pattern in solid apricot. A primula-motif chintz distinguishes the canopy, curtains, and pillows in the master bedroom; to unify the design, the canopy lining, in a dainty coral design, is repeated in the upholstery. And although Federal-era taste often leaned toward carpets with bold patterns, the delicate look of these interiors demanded, and received, a number of Oushak rugs in typically pale, fade-away tones that are as understated as the Philips House itself. ☞

OPPOSITE: IN A GUEST ROOM, A
QUILT'S CRISP COMPASS DESIGN AND
INTRICATE STITCHING COMPLEMENT THE
ATTENUATED LINES OF THE MAHOGANY FOUR-
POSTER BED WITH REEDED POSTS AND
CLASSICAL URN FINIALS.

ABOVE: THE ORIGINAL HEART-CARVED
MANTELPIECE SETS A LIGHT TONE FOR
THE MASTER BEDROOM, WHERE
QUILTS WITH PATCHES OF GOLD COORDINATE
WITH THE MATCHING FLORAL-PRINT
CANOPY AND CURTAIN FABRIC.

RIGHT: SIMPLICITY IS THE STATEMENT
IN THIS "GARRET" GUEST ROOM;
MATCHING PATCHWORK QUILTS TOP TWIN
19TH-CENTURY CANNONBALL BEDS.

southern *grace*

A DELIGHTFUL SENSE OF DELICACY PERVADES THIS two-story residence, built in the 1920s in suburban Atlanta. With its traditional detailing, the house exemplifies the Colonial Revival, a quintessential American style introduced in the late 1800s and still popular today. Yet while this type of architecture was based on 18th-century design — revival houses from the early 20th century in particular were often careful copies of Colonial buildings — the owner was not interested in adhering strictly to any one era. Instead, she chose to interpret the interiors freely. Indeed, the furnishings are not only from a range of periods but also from several countries.

RIGHT: THE NEED FOR COMFORT AND PRACTICALITY IN THE KITCHEN–FAMILY ROOM DOES NOT CONFLICT WITH ITS DELICATE MOOD. AN 18TH-CENTURY FRENCH SETTEE WITH VELVET UPHOLSTERY AND A FRENCH ARMCHAIR PROVIDE STYLISH SEATING. THE WOOL RUG, SPRINKLED WITH FLOWERS, IS DURABLE ENOUGH FOR HEAVY TRAFFIC.

BELOW: THIS INVITING SEATING AREA, CENTERED AROUND AN EBONY-INLAID TABLE ON A LYRE BASE, ANCHORS ONE END OF THE LARGE LIVING ROOM.

ABOVE AND OPPOSITE: AN ELEGANT COLOR SCHEME UNIFIES THE LIVING ROOM, WHERE THE MOTTLED APRICOT OF THE WALL GLAZE PULLS TOGETHER THE PINK, GOLD, AND BLUE TONES REPEATED IN THE UPHOLSTERY FABRICS AND RUG.

Whether French Rococo, English Regency, or Swedish Country, any style went, as long as it enhanced the light-as-air look.

As in all classic interiors, however, the rooms exhibit a comforting continuity — incorporating a predominantly pale but rich color palette, understated accessories, and graceful, curvilinear furniture throughout. The subtlety is intentional, meant to reflect the personality of the home-owner, a sophisticated traveler and collector. "She's a lovely lady," says the interior designer,

Dan Carithers, "and I wanted the house to be flattering to her gentle nature."

Generously though humanly scaled rooms, refined woodwork, and abundant windows provided the perfect structure for the desired look: pretty, colorful, and easy to live with. Part of that look involved allowing the outdoors to become a feature of the room. Relatively simple fabric treatments soften the linear window frames, bringing color and texture to the scheme without blocking the view. To further enhance

the natural light, the living and dining rooms were treated to "sunny" backgrounds. Apricot and yellow glazing lends a translucent glow to walls, accented by curtain fabrics in golds and pale corals. The bedrooms are more subdued, with simple striped wall coverings and textured rugs in neutral colors.

Another touch of the outdoors is provided by the abundant floral motifs, repeated in upholstery, carpets, pillow covers, bed linens, ceramic wares, paintings, and even the candelabra. Because flower patterns can sometimes appear overwhelming, the upholstery and other fabrics generally feature single blooms or small sprigs. Complementary toiles, plaids, and stripes also help keep the look simple and fresh.

The approach to furnishing the rooms is equally sensitive. In the dining room, for instance, Regency chairs with flared saber legs and spiral-turned top rails are a gentle presence, despite their black painted finish. Even the large table seems to soar, its circular top set on an open, cuplike base. ⌘

ABOVE: THE ONLY STRONG WALL COLOR IS IN THE HALL, WHERE A RICH PERSIMMON SETS OFF A SWEDISH PAINTED MIRROR.

BELOW: GILDED ACCESSORIES, INCLUDING AN 1800 ENGLISH PINWORK BOX AND A FRENCH CLOCK, CREATE A UNIFIED VIGNETTE.

OPPOSITE: A FRENCH CRYSTAL CHANDELIER AND LATE 18TH-CENTURY FRENCH GILT MIRROR SET THE TONE IN THE DINING ROOM, WHICH IS THE MOST FORMAL AND ELABORATE INTERIOR. SPIRAL TURNINGS ON THE REGENCY CHAIRS COMPLEMENT SIMILAR DETAILS ON THE MID-19TH-CENTURY ENGLISH MAHOGANY SIDEBOARD. THE RARE PAINTED CHINESE TEA CANISTERS ALSO DATE FROM THE 1800s.

past *and* present

A SMART USE OF SALVAGE, A THOROUGHGOING knowledge of early American design, and a collection of Colonial-era antiques have turned back the clock inside this 1980s brick ranch — by at least two centuries. Located near Louisville, the house was custom built by a couple who had spent some 50 years acquiring and studying furnishings not only from Kentucky but also from New England, the Mid-Atlantic, Europe, and Asia. With children grown and living away from home, the owners turned their attention to showcasing and tending their extended family of treasures.

The single-story residence is an ingenious example of how to bring Colonial feeling to a contemporary

OPPOSITE: A LARGE KEEPING ROOM RE-CREATES THE KITCHEN-CUM-GATHERING PLACE COMMON IN COLONIAL HOMES. EARLY AMERICAN IRONWARE INCLUDES ANDIRONS, POTS, AND A LONG-HANDLED PEEL FOR BAKING; HEARTH-SIDE SEATING IS PROVIDED BY A 19TH-CENTURY SETTLE AND A 17TH-CENTURY CARVER CHAIR.

ABOVE: FROM A COLLECTION OF 55 TILES, THESE DUTCH DELFT SQUARES BEAR A VARIETY OF MOTIFS, FROM GENRE SCENES TO BIBLE VERSES. THE PILLAR-AND-SCROLL CLOCK WAS MADE BY ELI TERRY AROUND 1830.

ABOVE: A VIVIDLY COLORED LINSEY-
WOOLSEY COVERLET AND BRIGHT ORIENTAL
RUGS WORK WELL WITH THE STRONG LINES
OF THE CHIPPENDALE CHAIRS AND QUEEN
ANNE HIGHBOY IN THIS GUEST ROOM.

BELOW: ONE OF THE HOMEOWNERS
DESIGNED THE MAPLE HALF-TESTER BEDS
AND ALSO SEWED THE CREWELWORK
SPREADS AND HANGINGS.

building and combine convenience with historic ambience. Among the modern features are spacious rooms, large windows, and a layout that offers both privacy and good traffic flow. Yet in every other respect, the house caters to the past, built from stone, brick, and architectural details salvaged from three 19th-century Louisville structures slated for demolition. Although new, the white-oak flooring replicates the broad tongue-and-groove planks characteristic of period homes; even the massive hearth beam was specially rough-hewn.

An authentic color scheme also plays an important role. Plastered walls painted "dirty" white echo the whitewash commonly used in the 18th century, while the strong trim colors were drawn from the favored Colonial palette of mustard yellow, sage green, and slate blue. As was fashionable in elegant colonial houses, vibrantly hued wool Oriental carpets figure prominently as well — covering not only floors but also tables.

OPPOSITE: DISTINGUISHED BY A MATCHING
VALANCE AND CANOPY IN A BARGELLO
PATTERN, COORDINATING WINDOW AND BED
HANGINGS BRING A FASHIONABLE COLONIAL
TOUCH TO THIS BEDROOM. THE CIRCA-1830S
GLASS-FRONT CHEST WITH ITS ORIGINAL
PANES WAS MADE IN KENTUCKY AND
EXEMPLIFIES THE SIMPLE, STURDY COUNTRY
FURNITURE OF THE REGION.

Against this backdrop is a careful assembly of antiques ranging in period from the Pilgrim era to the 19th century. Treasure hunts along the East Coast netted such first-class finds as a late 17th-century paneled chest from Virginia, a Carver chair and a Queen Anne cherry drop-leaf dining table from New England, and a set of splat-back chairs from the Hudson River Valley. Early American decorative objects, including Chinese Export porcelain and Dutch delft — both coveted in Colonial times — catch the eye and serve as important highlights in each room. ⇐⇒

ABOVE: THE LOOK IS VERY EARLY AMERICAN IN THE LIVING ROOM, WHERE BANNISTER-BACK CHAIRS, A TRUMPET-LEG WILLIAM AND MARY HIGHBOY, AND A CHERRY GATELEG TABLE REFLECT THE TASTE FOR HEAVILY TURNED FURNITURE PREVALENT AROUND 1700.

RIGHT: GRACEFUL QUEEN ANNE PIECES, INCLUDING AN ASSEMBLED SET OF CLASSIC VASE-SPLAT CHAIRS AND A FLAT-TOP HIGHBOY, PREDOMINATE IN THE DINING ROOM.

townhouse *style*

BEFITTING ITS ORIGINAL STATUS AS A DESIRABLE
Capitol Hill address in a district catering to 19th-
century congressmen and civil servants, this elegant
Washington, D.C., townhouse has been completely
renovated and redecorated with respect for its
architectural heritage. Fortunately, the "bones" were
already in place. Built in 1885, the two-story Italianate
structure boasted such traditional touches as arched
windows, marble fireplace mantels, and ornate
plaster moldings. After several years of stripping,
refinishing, and retouching, these original decorative
elements shine once again. When it came time to
"flesh out" the skeleton, the owner's personal taste

was the starting point. "He likes formality but not fussiness," says James Dean. The design and restoration specialist oversaw the project, which combines good antiques, beautiful finishes, and comfortable upholstered pieces to meet the owner's definition of an English country house.

The owner, who grew up with formal 18th-century furniture, gravitates naturally to the stately lines of Queen Anne and Chippendale styles and to the rich look of their woods. The cabriole-legged sideboard in the dining room and the bonnet-topped highboy in the front bedroom, for example, would have been at home in any Colonial house. He also appreciates the sophistication of cut-crystal chandeliers, damask pillows, and gilded mirror frames, all of which provide elegant accents. At the same time, flowing fabrics and plump sofas and chairs keep the interiors light and inviting. Simple, tailored swags dressing the windows are just enough to soften the shape and add color without obscuring the handsome moldings.

Scale was another consideration. Like many 19th-century residences in this city, this one was blessed with high ceilings — 11 feet— but the floor space was not so generous. The challenge was to select furnishings large enough to maintain a presence without overwhelming the rooms. Generously proportioned, boldly detailed pieces were the solution. The cherry table in the dining room, for example, can comfortably accommodate eight, and a mahogany tester bed with ornate posts that soar more than seven-and-one-half feet holds its own in the bedroom. To maximize natural light, always at a premium in attached townhouses, the walls here were coated in warm-hued paints: lemon yellow, pumpkin orange, and a vermilion that radiates like a summer sunset.

A particularly pleasing mix of the fine and formal extends to the accessories. While handsome collections of Chinese Export porcelain and Staffordshire take pride of place throughout the house, there was also room for such sentimental favorites as a 19th-century promotional pottery pitcher from a midwestern mill and a charming 1940s Bavarian cuckoo clock.

OPPOSITE AND BELOW: A SIMPLE IVORY COTTON SPREAD ON THE CIRCA-1820S ENGLISH MAHOGANY TESTER BED BECOMES A VISUAL ISLAND OF CALM IN A ROOM DOMINATED BY STRONG ELEMENTS. THE FLORAL-PRINT COTTON FABRIC OF THE BED HANGINGS AND CURTAINS, AS WELL AS THE ORIENTAL RUGS, PICKS UP THE BRILLIANT ORANGE-RED WALL COLOR. THE SCANDINAVIAN BRIDE'S CHEST AT THE FOOT OF THE BED IS INSCRIBED WITH THE BETROTHED'S INITIALS AND THE DATE 1856.

LEFT: AMONG THE HANDSOME
ACCESSORIES ON A SHERATON
CHERRY CANDLESTAND IS AN
OLD PARIS PORCELAIN
VEILLEUSE FROM 1810, USED
TO KEEP BEVERAGES WARM.

BELOW: OUR FOUNDING
FATHER, PORTRAYED IN A
MASONIC JACKET, PEERS DOWN
OVER A MAPLE CHIPPENDALE
CHEST FROM AROUND 1770.

classic *colonial*

SAMUEL PURCELL WAS A PROSPEROUS, ALBEIT parsimonious, miller and farmer in 1780, when he built a sturdy two-room stone house in northern Virginia. Although he did without closets and hallways — they would have been counted as taxable "rooms" — this practical Quaker nonetheless enlarged his home twice during the next 40 years and appointed it with features that reflected current fashions, such as paneled walls, turned balusters, cupboards with reeded decoration, and fireplace surrounds ornamented with urns and bellflowers.

By the 1990s, however, Rich Bottom Farm lay suffering from decades of neglect, although its

OPPOSITE: IN THE PARLOR,
A PAIR OF CHIPPENDALE
RIBBON-BACK CHAIRS, WHICH
WERE QUITE POPULAR IN POST-
REVOLUTIONARY AMERICA,
FLANK A 1770S FALL-FRONT
DESK FROM MASSACHUSETTS.
THE PILLAR-AND-SCROLL
CLOCK WAS MADE IN 1818.

features remained intact. The house was rescued by a couple who saw it as an ideal backdrop for their extensive collection of American furniture and decorative arts. In an effort that the thrifty Purcell would perhaps have approved, they undertook the restoration themselves with one guiding principle: to remain faithful to the original construction and return each section to its period. The key to understanding an old house, they say, is simplicity. "If you observe carefully, the house will tell you what to do."

Once they had uncovered the "high-country" charm that had been buried beneath linoleum flooring and layers of wallpaper, the couple restored the original elements to perfection. They hand-scrubbed the chestnut and heart-pine floors, rebuilt pegged windows, and even repaired the "horsehair" plaster, white-washed in the manner common in Purcell's day.

Against this simple background, the furnishings stand out all the more, and each section of the farmstead is allowed to display its own personality. The earliest part comprises the keeping room—kitchen and an upstairs guest room, originally a communal sleeping loft; both have exposed rafters and a decidedly down-home, colonial feeling. Featuring the original 14-foot-long stone fireplace, the kitchen is furnished with

BELOW: EARLY 1800s SHELF CLOCKS WITH ÉGLOMISÉ DECORATION ARE GROUPED ABOVE THE CAMELBACK SOFA. THE ONLY TOUCH OF WALLPAPER IS A TOBACCO-LEAF BORDER THAT REFERS TO THE AGRICULTURAL HERITAGE OF THE REGION.

OPPOSITE: THIS GUEST ROOM, IN THE EARLIEST SECTION OF THE HOUSE (1780), IS OUTFITTED WITH SIMPLE COUNTRY PIECES, INCLUDING A MAPLE QUEEN ANNE HIGHBOY FROM CONNECTICUT AND A 1770s CHERRY CORNER CHAIR MADE IN VIRGINIA.

an 18th-century pine tavern table and Windsor seating pieces that accentuate the early American look.

Encompassing the dining room and an upstairs parlor, the 1801 section is slightly fancier, distinguished by more refined detailing, evident in the dining-room fireplace surround designed with ornamental pilasters and sunburst motifs. Here an early 19th-century cherry-topped table features elaborately turned legs of lustrous mahogany. An equally graceful chandelier custom crafted for the house in hand-cut Czech crystal provides the lighting.

The most formal section of Purcell's expanding house was built in 1820 and now contains the master bedroom and the main parlor, appointed with stylish furniture from the Chippendale and Federal periods.

The owners' penchant for rescue and rehabilitation comes together in another form noticeable in every room: a collection of 50 clocks that they repaired themselves. Among them are examples from such noted New England makers as Seth Thomas, Eli Terry, and Simon Willard — one of whose first tall-case clocks, with elaborate fretwork, stands in the parlor. ⊂═►

THE EXPOSED RAFTERS IN THE 1801 DINING ROOM DO NOT
CONFLICT WITH THE OVERALL ELEGANT FEEL ESTABLISHED BY
THE TURNED-LEGGED CHERRY-AND-MAHOGANY TABLE, RIBBON-BACK
CHAIRS, AND TWO-TIERED MAHOGANY DUMBWAITER.
THE RETICULATED BASKETS ON THE TABLE, SERVING PIECES
ON THE DUMBWAITER, AND URNS ON THE MANTEL ARE
PART OF AN EXTENSIVE COLLECTION OF OLD PARIS PORCELAIN —
LUXURY WARES MADE BY SEVERAL FACTORIES IN THAT
CITY IN THE LATE 1700s AND EARLY 1800s.

RIGHT: INCISED
LACQUER NESTING TABLES
FROM CHINA ADD ORIENTAL
FLAIR TO THE MIX.

BELOW: LOUIS XV SIDE
CHAIRS IN EMBOSSED VELVET
AND A MARBLE-TOPPED GILT
CONSOLE DISPLAY MID-18TH-
CENTURY FRENCH TASTE
IN THE ENTRY HALL.

OPPOSITE: DUSKY LACQUERED
WALLS IN THE LIVING ROOM
SET OFF A PAIR OF LOUIS XVI
ARMCHAIRS AND A LUXURIOUS
DOWN-FILLED SOFA.
THE MARBLE-AND-ORMOLU
INCENSE BURNERS NEXT TO
THE MIRROR ARE 18TH-CENTURY
PIECES FROM FRANCE.

urban *refinement*

CLARE FRASER BELIEVES IN ROOMS THAT "COSSET" their inhabitants, indulging them in luxurious surroundings that depend on clever color palettes and sumptuous materials to strike a formal yet welcoming mood. Reflecting a professional's experienced eye, the interior designer's own Manhattan apartment is infused with a nostalgia for Old World elegance — a calm oasis where classic European furniture, cool marble, rich velvets, and gleaming mirrors create a refuge from the fast pace of city living.

To achieve the look she wanted, Fraser was willing to start from scratch, given the right location: a home on a pretty, old-fashioned New York street

lined with brownstones and trees. The spacious seven-room apartment she found met the location criterion, but it was a plain-vanilla box lacking any architectural distinction. Building up the shell required yards of elaborate cornice moldings, which were often used in combination, as in the egg-and-dart, modillion, and water-lily motif designs that give dimension to the living room. Doors were custom made of warm mahogany, and fluted pilasters and raised paneling covered soffits and niches to supply the architectural character that was so sorely missing.

Equally dramatic are some of the wall treatments, even though they are rendered in a neutral palette. In the living room, for instance, surfaces lacquered in layers of a dusky, glossy gray glow with great depth; space-expanding mirrors fitted in an end wall reflect the glow. Another sophisticated paint finish is the marbling in the entry hall, where creamy beige walls are veined with dark green, then framed with a three-inch faux-marble border.

OPPOSITE: THE PINE-PANELED LIBRARY OFFERS A CHOICE OF COMFORTABLE SPOTS FOR BOOK BROWSING, INCLUDING CHINTZ-COVERED SLIPPER CHAIRS AND A LOUIS XV WALNUT ARMCHAIR.

ABOVE: THE LIBERAL USE OF TOILE LENDS CONTINUITY TO THE FAMILY ROOM.

BELOW: A SWEET AND SOOTHING PLACE TO REST, THE GUEST ROOM FEATURES WALL FABRIC, CURTAINS, AND BED SKIRT IN A COUNTRY FRENCH PRINT.

ABOVE: THE SHIELD-BACK DINING CHAIRS,
PAINTED WITH PRETTY FEDERAL-ERA SWAGS,
WERE MADE IN PORTUGAL IN THE 1970S.

BELOW: RUSSIAN CHINA MADE IN THE 1800S,
ETCHED SWEDISH GOBLETS, AND FANCY SILVER
FLATWARE SET A SOPHISTICATED TABLE.

Soothing to both touch and eye, fabrics range from a formal embossed velvet to a casual chintz. Skilled in mating unexpected patterns, Fraser helped bring order to an array of designs with a few classic tricks, such as covering the largest piece in a room in a plain fabric or repeating the same fabric throughout a space. In the family room, a busy toile appears on the walls, draperies, chairs, and pillows; the geometric carpet and a plaid chair thus work as accents and do not compete with the predominant print.

Perfectly suited to the sophisticated setting is the furniture, which hails primarily from France and encompasses the curvaceous consoles and armchairs favored in Louis XV's era, as well as the more symmetrical chests and *bergères* associated with his successor. Oriental decorative arts, including porcelain Fo dogs, and a famille verte urn-turned-lamp are completely compatible accents.

OPPOSITE: INTIMATE DINNERS TAKE PLACE
AROUND AN 18TH-CENTURY RUSSIAN TABLE
SWATHED IN STRIPED SILK; A CREAM
SILK-LOOK STRIPED COTTON COVERS THE
WALLS. NATURAL LIGHT FILTERS THROUGH
FILMY SHEER DRAPERIES TRIMMED WITH
GILDED WOODEN TASSELS.

CHAPTER TWO Color and pattern are an inseparable and indispensable pair in any interior. Whether provided by a bold splash of paint on a wall, a demure checked cushion on a chair, or even the precise arrangement of china on a cupboard shelf, these two elements do more than any others to set the scene.

Where do classic colors and patterns come from? Everywhere. The same forest green or buff gold that colonists once favored for painting their woodwork can still bring trim to life. The same scenic wallpaper patterns that were fashionable in the Federal era are still elegant choices for a formal dining room. And the same exotic paisley designs that 19th-century women once draped over their shoulders on shawls can today swathe a table in style.

Yet beyond paint, paper, and fabric there are countless other sources for these fundamental elements of design. The silhouette of a candlestick on a fireplace mantel, the shapes of windows in a wall, and the line of throw pillows on a sofa all create distinctive patterns. In a similar manner, a

color & pattern

stack of bandboxes arranged on a chest or a group of cobalt goblets on a table can contribute important touches of color to catch the eye.

Color and pattern affect not only the eye but also the mood and mind. Bright, vivid, contrasting colors and complex patterns churn up excitement, whereas soft, complementary tones and small-scale, simple motifs cast a more calming spell. Orderly, repeated patterns and carefully controlled palettes appear more formal, while freewheeling or unexpected juxtapositions seem casual. Color and pattern also have practical applications: using an eye-popping paint color is a clever way to accentuate an exquisitely carved molding, and a complex stencil pattern disguises irregularities in a time-worn floor.

Perhaps the greatest asset of this indomitable pair is their ability to turn back the clock. Something as simple as painting a checkerboard on a floor or spreading a patchwork quilt on a bed not only helps make an ordinary room remarkable but also establishes an immediate visual connection to design traditions with deep roots in the American past.

past *inspirations*

in a midwestern suburb

THE STRONG COLORS AND BOLD PATTERNS of early American interiors can bring character to houses from any era. Consider this comfortable home in Indianapolis: although it was built in the 1960s, the rooms have been "aged" with the reds, golds, and greens favored some two centuries ago. The prevailing palette — a traditional Colonial scheme of whitewashed walls accented with wood-work in dark tones — is not absolutely "correct" in terms of historic authenticity, but that is the point.

Rather than trying to slavishly duplicate an 18th-century interior, the owners merely borrowed elements that lend a period look, "making the most" of what

FURNISHINGS WITH CLASSIC GEOMETRIC DESIGNS, SUCH AS A
STRIPED RAG RUG AND A PIN-DOT-PATTERNED LOLLING CHAIR,
STRIKE THE RIGHT BALANCE IN THE LIVING ROOM;
CANTON AND IMARI PLATES PROVIDE ACCENTS IN BLUE.

they had. In many cases, this spirit of improvisation involved mixing trim colors inspired by the paint finishes of the antique furnishings at hand. The rich leaf green of the living room paneling, for instance, was custom blended to match a small door from an old cupboard that has been incorporated into the overmantel. And the original apple-green paint of the large Irish shoefoot dish dresser in the parlor prompted the color scheme of the compasslike floor design, framed against a bright red background.

The pine flooring also becomes a canvas of sorts in the dining room, where a checkerboard floor combines the taupe of the dado with a vibrant salmon red, all contained — and tamed by — a border in soft fawn. ⌦

LEFT: THE BACKDROP IN THE DINING ROOM IS A STRONG BUT WARM COLOR SCHEME OF SPANISH YELLOW AND A SOFTER TAUPE THAT IS REPEATED IN THE CHECKERBOARD FLOOR PATTERN TO UNIFY THE SPACE. SIMPLE FURNISHINGS, SUCH AS THE ENGLISH DISH RACK FILLED WITH PEWTER PLATES, COMPLEMENT THE DECOR WITHOUT COMPETING.

BELOW: THE MOTTLED SURFACE OF THE ORIGINAL PAINT FINISH ON THE 18TH-CENTURY FOOD CUPBOARD, KNOWN AS A LIVERY CUPBOARD, BLENDS PERFECTLY WITH THE REST OF THE ROOM.

OPPOSITE: WHILE FAVORING INTENSE PAINT COLORS, THE OWNERS TOOK A SUBTLER APPROACH WITH PATTERN, RELYING MAINLY ON THE SIMPLE GEOMETRY OF MOLDINGS AND THE SILHOUETTES OF EARLY AMERICAN ANTIQUES TO PROVIDE INTEREST. BLACK-PAINTED AND BOLDLY SHAPED 18TH-CENTURY FURNISHINGS IN THE PARLOR STAND OUT WELL AGAINST THE BRIGHT COLORS OF THE ROOM. ADAPTED FROM AN EARLY 18TH-CENTURY HOUSE IN MASSACHUSETTS, THE FLOOR DESIGN SERVES AS A PAINTED "RUG."

historic *patterns*
in a New England village

IN THE EARLY 1800s DAWNED A NEW AGE FOR
interiors — light, bright, and airy, with a decidedly
Continental accent — and families of means were
no longer content to live with the deep colors
and heavy patterns associated with the English-
influenced design of the previous century. It was in
this spirit that Hinsdale Williams, one of the
wealthiest landowners in the Connecticut River
Valley, used fancy Federal features to "modernize"
the Georgian-style home he had inherited around
1820. Among the most elegant components of the
Williams House, now a museum at Historic
Deerfield, Inc., are the wallpapers, all precise

LIGHT PAINT COLORS
AND PRONOUNCED PATTERNS
DISTINGUISH THE
WILLIAMS HOUSE,
A FEDERAL-ERA RESTORATION
AT HISTORIC DEERFIELD,
IN MASSACHUSETTS. THE STAR-
AND-MOON PAPER REPLICATES
A 19TH-CENTURY DESIGN.

reproductions or original to the residence. The dining-room paper, for example, replicates one manufactured in Boston in the early 1800s and boasts a faux-drapery pattern. Such illusionistic papers, inspired by French designs produced between the late 1700s and the 1830s, were meant to create the effect of yards of luxurious fabrics shirred softly on the walls. The 1815 French paper in the formal north parlor exemplifies the scenic patterns also much in vogue at the time.

Federal-era floors were often as eye-catching as the walls, and the house boasts two typical richly patterned examples: a floorcloth with a popular lozenge design (page 67) and a fine Brussels carpet, a type of loop-pile carpet that was usually installed wall to wall. Characteristically, it bears a large-scale floral design — to ensure that this luxury item would be noticed.

OPPOSITE: REPRODUCING AN 1810 ENGLISH PATTERN, THE CHINTZ USED FOR BED DRESSINGS WAS CHOSEN TO COORDINATE WITH A FLORAL WALLPAPER THAT REPLICATES A DESIGN FROM AROUND 1820.

RIGHT: LARGE-SCALE PATTERNS IN SHADES OF GRAY-GREEN ARE FOUND IN THE NORTH PARLOR. THE BRUSSELS CARPET REPRODUCES A CIRCA-1820 ENGLISH DESIGN. THE FRENCH WALLPAPER, ORIGINAL TO THE HOUSE, DATES TO AROUND 1815.

farmhouse *chic*

in a city setting

UNABLE TO MOVE TO THE COUNTRY, THE OWNERS of this Manhattan apartment simply invited the colors and classic woodwork designs of an 18th-century New England farmhouse into the city. Since the interiors were completely featureless, they welcomed a complete transformation. In particular, the interior designer, Matt Larkin, used architecture to bring in bands of color, both "horizontally and vertically," as well as to create pattern. Chair rails and crown moldings that stop about a foot short of the ceiling line give dimension to the tall expanses of blank wall — a neat trick that simultaneously makes ceilings appear loftier and living spaces

ACID GREEN DOMINATES
A LIVELY COLOR SCHEME ACCENTED WITH
PINKS AND REDS.

more intimate. An arched bookshelf reminiscent of an 18th-century corner cupboard and a curved valance also turned the static block of living-room windows into a more dynamic shape. Perhaps the most stunning transformation involved creating a fireplace where there once was none. Constructed of 1700s brick, this period feature is based on a classic colonial pattern: multilayered mantel shelf, paneled overmantel, and fluted pilasters.

Throughout the apartment, the woodwork was painted in deep, bold, 18th-century colors such as pine green and slate blue — applied primarily as glazes for a cleaner, more delicate look that reflects light and creates depth. The translucent quality of the glazes works particularly well as a softer backdrop for the furnishings, which include a number of antiques with strong paint colors, richly patterned Oriental rugs, a salmon-colored wing chair, and an armchair covered in a complex chintz print. ☞

LEFT AND ABOVE: SALMON-COLORED UPHOLSTERY MAKES AN EYE-CATCHING CONTRAST WITH GREEN PANELING AND BROWN FIREPLACE PILASTERS, DETAILED WITH FAUX MARBLING. HALLWAY WALLS ARE WASHED A SLIGHTLY DEEPER OCHER THAN THOSE OF THE LIVING ROOM, AND THE TRIM IS PAINTED A DARKER GREEN.

OPPOSITE: THE BEDROOM FEATURES A SOOTHING COLOR SCHEME OF CREAM AND DARK BLUE.

SO SUPERBLY COORDINATED AS TO APPEAR effortlessly tossed together, patterns predominate in this stylish Long Island weekend retreat. Pattern adds activity, movement, and life, says the owner, designer Charlotte Moss. "You can't be squeamish about experimenting with it. You have to play." And play she did, mixing florals and geometrics until she achieved the relaxed yet refined atmosphere she wanted for a country house frequently filled with family and guests.

One principle remained constant throughout: as long as the color and scale of the patterns were compatible, contrasting designs could be layered

MIX BUT DON'T MATCH IS THE GUIDING PRINCIPLE OF THIS TABLE SETTING, WHERE ENGLISH BLUE-AND-WHITE CHINA, AMERICAN PRESSED-GLASS STEMWARE, AND SILVER CUTLERY IN DIFFERENT PATTERNS PLAY OFF THE VIBRANT DESIGNS OF OVERLAPPING PAISLEY SHAWLS.

with abandon. In the dining room, for example, two distinctive wallpaper patterns — a tone-on-tone damask above the chair rail and a subtle cream stripe below — are unified by their soft ocher color. The same golden tones repeat on the tabletop, where a pair of 19th-century paisley shawls becomes a centerpiece aswirl with lively shapes. The sinuous scrolls of the paisley motif in turn play off the exuberant patterns of the antique English blue-and-white tableware, whose colors are echoed in cobalt-blue goblets.

The level of patterning in the living room is less intense yet equally effective. In a dramatic space with soaring walls, the designer made the dimensions more manageable by hanging fabric "curtains" about halfway up the wall. The muted floral pattern of the draperies and deep swags in a cool celadon tempers the warm burgundy color of striped and other patterns.

The scheme for the master bedroom is a soothing blend of aqua blue and rose, which appear alone or together in all the patterns. "In some rooms you want the patterns to be strong," says Moss, "but here I wanted them easy on the eye." The creamy hues of the walls and floor make these large surfaces appear to recede, so the bed becomes the center of attention. The medium-sized checked pattern of the canopy, hangings, and skirt coordinates with the similarly scaled floral designs on the 1920s American coverlet and contemporary pillow shams. A Chinese needlepoint carpet and a bedside cupboard custom made to incorporate antique painted wall panels from France carry the floral motif into the room. ⌐⊶

whimsy *in paint*
in a Nantucket cottage

TROMPE L'OEIL AND WHIMSICAL SCENIC PAINTING play a major role in boosting the already considerable charm of this historic 1776 house on Nantucket Island, a former whaling port off the Massachusetts coast. The focal point of the cottage is the entry hall and adjacent stairwell — an often awkward, angular space that here becomes a clever study in pattern and perspective.

Following in the footsteps of New England's itinerant ornamental painters, a local artist has adorned the walls with a folksy landscape: in this case, scenes of Nantucket as it may have appeared around the mid-19th century.

INSPIRED BY
ANTIQUE PRINTS AND
PAINTINGS, THE ENTRY
HALL MURAL DEPICTS
A SCENE OF BYGONE
ISLAND LIFE.

The charm heightens as one ascends the stairs to the vantage point of an angular bluff and is offered a vista of farms, harbor, and countryside; the stair treads themselves are painted a deep green, so that "spectators" feel as if they are standing on a grassy hill.

Whimsy also found a place in a bedroom, where plaster walls are patterned to look like dressed and pointed stone. The trompe l'oeil design, in warm tans and grays, not only features the striations of the natural material it mimics but also appears to be subtly weathered, as if the surface had been bleached and battered over centuries by the harsh elements. In the sitting room, attention shifts to the floor, where a large-scale diamond pattern completes the conceit by affecting the look of costly marble tiles — recalling a fashion particularly popular in the late 18th century.

OPPOSITE: A NEOCLASSICAL PIER TABLE AND GILDED MIRROR, BOTH DATING FROM ABOUT 1820, WORK WELL WITH A FAUX-STONE BEDROOM-WALL PATTERN THAT HAS VAGUE OVERTONES OF ANCIENT GREEK OR ROMAN ARCHITECTURE.

RIGHT: A UNIFIED COLOR THEME OF RUSSET RED ALLOWS THE CHECKERBOARD FLOOR TO BE THE MOST PROMINENT ELEMENT IN THE SITTING ROOM.

Elements of design
faux finishes

ABOVE LEFT AND LEFT: THE ORIGINAL
PAINTWORK SURVIVES IN THE 1802
TENNESSEE FRONTIER MANSION
CRAGFONT. BOLD BRUSHWORK APPEARS ON
THE STAIR RISERS AND THE OVERMANTEL,
WHICH IS COMPLETE WITH A FANCIFUL
FAUX BORDER THAT WOULD HAVE "FRAMED"
A PAINTING IN THE CENTRAL PANEL.

ABOVE: HAMPTON HALL, AN OPULENT 1783
ESTATE NEAR BALTIMORE, FEATURES A
FAUX-PAINTED DOOR MEANT TO MIMIC
SATINWOOD INLAY AND THREE DIFFERENT
TYPES OF MAHOGANY, INCLUDING FLAME
VENEER, IN THE RAISED PANELS.

EARLY AMERICAN SETTLERS WERE GENERALLY AN ingenious lot — and few more so than the 18th- and 19th-century homeowners whose tastes for color and pattern exceeded their pocketbooks or the materials at hand. A fancy marble mantel too costly? They would simply paint plain wood to imitate precious stone. No mahogany available for the parlor door? They would simply "grain" a surface until it resembled an exotic hardwood.

Then, as now, paint was the great ingredient of alchemy for changing a room. If used cleverly, it could not only give one material the appearance of another but also make even a modest farmhouse appear to belong to a family of means.

Such faux, or false, finishes were applied throughout an interior: on fireplace surrounds

and overmantels, stair risers, doors, window trim, built-in cupboards, floors, chair rails, wainscoting, even entire walls. The magicians responsible for this sleight of hand were usually itinerant ornamental painters, or "decorators," who traded their handwork for bed and board and a bit of money. Although they may have occasionally painted a portrait or landscape, they were primarily craftsmen who used their skills to fulfill practical needs rather than express a personal artistic vision. Often working with primitive tools, they could create marblelike veining with the mere feathery flick of a brush or impart the subtle gradations associated with wood grain by dragging a special type of comb over wet paint.

Realism was a prized achievement in faux finishes, but there was also room for "failure" and fantasy. Indeed, the earnest, although not always successful, attempts of an artisan to conjure expensive tiger maple from common pine often make the finished product all the more appealing. And painters who could not resist improving on nature by adding personal fillips and flourishes created works of art that are prized in interiors today. ←

THE 17-ROOM SAN FRANCISCO PLANTATION
HOUSE IN LOUISIANA IS ONE OF THE MOST
FLAMBOYANT ANTEBELLUM MANSIONS
IN THE CITY. COMPLETED IN 1856, THE
INTERIORS ARE ABLAZE WITH VIBRANT
COLORS AND PAINTED DECORATION.
THE GENTLEMEN'S PARLOR, DIRECTLY OFF
THE FOYER, FEATURES A STRIKING TRICK:
A WALL OF FOUR DOORS IS PAINTED
TO RESEMBLE A CLASSICAL FRESCO,
WITH ARABESQUE PANELS SYMBOLIZING
THE FOUR SEASONS.

Elements of design
stenciled designs

ABOVE LEFT AND ABOVE: MOSES EATON IS ONE OF THE FEW AMERICAN STENCIL PAINTERS OF THE EARLY 1800S WHOSE NAME AND WORK ARE DOCUMENTED. ORIGINAL DESIGNS HAVE BEEN PRESERVED IN THIS NEW HAMPSHIRE DINING ROOM, PAINTED IN EATON'S SIGNATURE SCHEME OF RED AND GREEN, WITH SUCH TYPICAL PERIOD MOTIFS AS LEAVES AND THE WEEPING WILLOW, A SYMBOL OF MOURNING.

LEFT: WITH THEIR CLASSICAL OVERTONES, SWAGS WERE A FAVORITE EARLY 19TH-CENTURY DESIGN. THIS STENCILED ENTRY HALL FEATURES THE MOTIF BOTH IN A ROSE-PATTERNED CORNICE FRIEZE AND IN GARLANDS STRETCHED BETWEEN URNS ALONG THE BASEBOARD.

LIKE FAUX FINISHES, STENCILED DESIGNS WERE originally devised to bring a touch of luxury into the home. During the 18th and 19th centuries, stenciling on walls was just a Yankee simplification of the same process used in hand painting the expensive, intricately patterned wallpapers manufactured in Europe. American decorative painters, however, often lacked the skill and time (itinerants were paid per project) to re-create complex designs. Instead, these practical artisans merely reduced popular motifs to basic shapes by cutting patterns from heavy paper and dabbing paint over these stencils with stiff, rounded brushes.

Just as wallpaper would adorn the "best" rooms, so stenciling was used mainly in the parlor or dining room. The look of contemporary wallpaper was carefully observed and imitated. Patterns were arranged in vertical rows that suggested strips of paper and often featured friezes along with door, window, chair rail, and baseboard borders. Among the favorite repeat motifs, all highly stylized, were flowers and foliage, geometric shapes, hearts, and stars. Eagles, weeping willows, pineapples, and flower baskets turn up in larger-scale, stand-alone designs often placed between two windows or on an overmantel. A popular frieze motif is the swag, which not only offered the touch of Classical ornament beloved in the Federal era but also suggested the folds of draped fabric that might be seen on the walls in affluent households.

Colors were equally simple and clean. Atop a fresh coat of whitewash, sometimes softly tinted, the stencil designs glowed in deeper reds, greens, ocher, and black. The colors were often mixed by the painters themselves from such pigment-rich materials as clays, brick dust, and lampblack.

printed *wallpaper*

ABOVE: WITH ITS LUSH PLANTINGS, THE
MYTHIC LANDSCAPE OF "ELDORADO" WAS
FEATURED IN A SCENIC PAPER ISSUED IN
1849 BY JEAN ZUBER & CIE, ONE OF
THE FOREMOST FIRMS IN FRANCE.

RIGHT: THIS HAND-PAINTED PAPER IS
A MODERN VERSION OF A "BIRD AND
FLOWER" PATTERN, ONE OF THREE
TRADITIONAL CHINESE DESIGN CATEGORIES.

BELOW: THE JOSEPH WEBB FAMILY HAD
THIS WOOL-FLOCKED PAPER HUNG IN ITS
WETHERSFIELD, CONNECTICUT, HOUSE IN
PREPARATION FOR THE 1781 VISIT OF
GENERAL GEORGE WASHINGTON.

An innovation in color and pattern that counted among the most coveted amenities in the colonial and Federal periods, wallpaper was introduced to the Colonies around 1700. The first papers, imported from England, were such a novelty that they were manufactured only in small sheets measuring roughly two by two-and-a-half feet; rolls became available around the 1730s. Although many early papers were patterned, usually in imitation of textiles, a solid-colored blue or green paper trimmed with a gilt border was considered quite stylish as well.

By the mid-1700s, however, the fashion was decidedly for figural designs. Imported primarily from England, the papers might be flocked with wool in an attempt to simulate sumptuous damask or velvet but were more commonly hand painted or "stampt" with repeat patterns ranging from dainty flower sprigs to imposing architectural colonnades. Particularly desirable were chinoiserie designs, whether on the authentic painted scenic papers produced in China and exported to the West, or on the sometimes faithful — sometimes charmingly clumsy — Western interpretations of the Eastern designs.

When it came to scenic wallpaper, however, none could compete with the brilliant hues and sophisticated floral and allegorical patterns of French papers, first imported to America in the 1780s. Those depicting entire panoramas of exotic landscapes, mythological tales, and historic events were the most desirable, especially for large-scale rooms. With typical initiative, Americans began producing papers based on the European imports as early as the 1750s. Although American designs included the ever-popular floral, geometric, scenic, and architectural motifs, they also offered such patriotic subjects as the Declaration of Independence and scenes memorializing President Washington's death. ←

LEFT: FORMER FIRST LADY ELIZABETH MONROE BROUGHT SOPHISTICATED TASTE TO ASH LAWN-HIGHLAND, THE VIRGINIA ESTATE SHE AND HER HUSBAND, JAMES, BUILT IN THE 1790S. ORIGINALLY HUNG WITH TAPESTRIES, THE DRAWING ROOM TODAY IS PAPERED WITH A HUNTING LANDSCAPE PRODUCED IN 1830 BY JEAN ZUBER & CIE.

BELOW: AN 1815 FRENCH SCENIC WALLPAPER DEPICTS A ROMANTICIZED NEOCLASSICAL SETTING.

OPPOSITE: ANOTHER IDYLLIC SCENE WITH CLASSICAL ARCHITECTURE IS SEEN IN THIS FRENCH "TERRACE OF ENCHANTMENT" PAPER.

painted *trim*

ABOVE LEFT: A RICH APPLE GREEN
RE-CREATES THE ORIGINAL TRIM COLOR IN
THIS FEDERAL-PERIOD PARLOR. STANDING
OUT AGAINST A WHITE PLASTER WALL,
THE SOLID HUE CALLS ATTENTION
TO THE CARVED DENTILS AND MOLDINGS
OF THE MANTELPIECE.

ABOVE: THIS SIMPLE TEXAS HOUSE BUILT
IN 1835 CONTAINED BUT TWO MAIN ROOMS,
ONE OF WHICH WAS THE PARLOR. AS THE
ONLY ARCHITECTURAL DETAIL OF NOTE, THE
FIREPLACE WAS PAINTED AN INTENSE BLUE,
WHICH IS REPEATED AT THE CORNICE LINE.

LEFT: A BUILT-IN CORNER CUPBOARD LIKE
THIS 1752 EXAMPLE WAS A VALUED BIT OF
CABINETWORK IN THE 18TH CENTURY. THE
CONTRASTING PAINT SCHEME HIGHLIGHTS
THE SIGNIFICANT FEATURES: REEDED
PILASTERS, A SHELL-CARVED DOME, AND
SCALLOPED SHELVES.

PAINTING PLASTER AND PANELING FIRST BECAME the rage in the second quarter of the 18th century. However, as early as the late 1600s, it was the fashion to highlight doors, windows, and finish molding with color. Painting woodwork served several purposes. First and foremost, it brought color into the house. But it also concealed inexpensive woods that offered few, if any, decorative features and called attention to important architectural details, such as mantelpieces and paneled dados.

While paint supplies were initially limited, dealers began appearing in major American cities around the 1720s. Colors were far from the somber, "sad" tones often associated with Colonial decorating. Indeed, they were often surprisingly, stunningly vibrant and were sometimes used in seemingly shocking combinations: a mid-1700s built-in cupboard might be painted turquoise or olive green, with salmon shelves or cornice detailing. Such vivid colors — sometimes applied in a highly desirable glossy finish — appeared more conspicuous in the often dim light of early colonial homes. Colors became tamer and more "tasteful" in the post-Revolutionary era, when pastels predominated. Yet even in the late 1700s and early 1800s, trim might still gleam with a sea green or apricot yellow. ←

LEFT: THE WOODWORK IN A 1710 MAINE HOUSE WAS ORIGINALLY DARK RED, BUT IN KEEPING WITH THE CONTEMPORARY TASTE FOR LIGHTER INTERIORS, IT WAS REPAINTED AROUND 1770 IN A MUSTARD GOLD THAT COORDINATES WITH BUFF YELLOW WALLS.

Elements of design
patterned *floors*

ABOVE LEFT: IN COLONIAL DAYS, FLOORCLOTHS WERE CONSIDERED FASHIONABLE FOR EVEN THE FINEST HOMES. THIS OPTICALLY INTRICATE EXAMPLE LIES IN THE MAIN PASSAGEWAY OF THE 1790 RICHMOND ESTATE, BUILT BY JOHN MARSHALL, ONE OF THE FIRST SUPREME COURT JUSTICES.

ABOVE: THE TULIP-PATTERN BORDER OF THIS STENCILED FLOOR IS REMINISCENT OF CARPET EDGING, WHILE THE DIAMONDS IMITATE STONE SLABS.

LEFT: A PAINTED COMPASS ROSE IS SURROUNDED BY SUBTLE VEINING SUGGESTING MARBLE.

Providing decorative interest underfoot, a painted floor not only will camouflage imperfections in an old or blemished surface but can also have the same design impact as a rug or patterned floor. The Colonial fashion for decorated floors, in fact, originated in an effort to imitate the various treatments found in the homes of wealthy colonists in the 1700s. Among these were floors of elegant stone pavers, as well as of wood inlaid with precious species such as mahogany and ebony. Large Oriental carpets also decked the "best" rooms and lay in smaller versions at bedside.

Imitating inlaid wood or even stone was merely a matter of painting directly on the floor planks. Indeed, the diamond or lozenge design often applied to 18th-century floors — and still so popular today — was simply an attempt to replicate the pattern of alternating marble tiles at less expense than the true stone. To suggest the patterns of woven rugs, the same painters who decorated walls would stencil geometric and floral motifs on the floor as well.

Starting around the 1720s, householders could also obtain floorcloths. These economical painted "carpets" were both imported from England and produced domestically in what became a widespread industry in the mid-1700s. Floorcloths were but another creative, practical means of bringing color and pattern into a room. Constructed of durable canvas, they were stenciled or hand painted to resemble carpeting or stone; popular designs included faux-marble patterns and geometric or figured motifs. In summer, the canvas cloths might be used to replace heavier pile carpets. And because they could withstand sweeping and scrubbing well, they found their way into dining rooms, hallways, and other areas subject to heavy wear or messy spills. ⬿

BELOW: THE DESIGN OF THIS GEOMETRIC FLOORCLOTH WAS ADAPTED FROM AN EARLY 19TH-CENTURY WALLPAPER PATTERN. LIKE MANY PERIOD FLOORCLOTHS AND CARPETS, IT FEATURES A BORDER AROUND THE CENTRAL FIELD AND INDIVIDUAL MOTIFS AT THE CORNERS. LARGE CANVAS FLOOR COVERINGS WERE TYPICALLY ATTACHED DIRECTLY TO THE FLOORBOARDS WITH TACKS.

CHAPTER THREE Fabrics and textiles were highly prized in Colonial times, and their position of honor in American decorating has not changed over the centuries. Because fabrics can underscore mood, usher in the seasons, accentuate a range of looks, and emphasize — or even alter — shapes, they are among the most useful decorating "tools" available. What better way to disguise a well-worn table, dress up an inexpensive chair, transform a fussy sofa, or make a boring bed seem less sleepy?

When it comes to devising a classic American look, fabrics and textiles contribute in several fundamental ways. First, their patterns instantly evoke an era: the simple blue-and-white check of homespun or the dazzling flame motif of bargello needlework belong as surely in a Colonial-style room as the scenic prints of toile do in a Federal interior.

Using a fabric for a particular treatment has similar power. Cloak a tester bed with a matching canopy, curtains, and coverlet, for example, and the look is 18th century. Hang formal swags in the windows, and the time advances to the 19th century.

fabric & textiles

For all of these reasons, it is important to consider carefully your choice of window curtains, bed dressings, upholstery, and slipcovers, and to think about how both the fabric and the way it is used affects a treatment and accents the style set by other furnishings in a room. A precise cut and smart tailoring will scribe a clean, economical line, while loose draping and layering lend a look of luxury. For formal effects, there are solid-colored velvets and tone-on-tone silk damasks; for a casual look, a printed cotton or a nubby linen might be just right.

Fortunately, such American favorites are available in a wealth of traditional designs, ranging from simple stripes and plaids to florals and scenic patterns. Many of the most popular are reproductions of early American patterns that still appear fresh and stylish today. Successful decorating with fabric, however, also invites improvisation. It is entirely acceptable to "break the rules" by letting bed hangings pool on the floor or trimming a slipcover with exaggerated bow ties. If the approach is thoughtful and the accents tasteful, the look will always be classic. ☞

history *preserved*
in a Tidewater plantation

IN THIS HISTORIC VIRGINIA FARMSTEAD, BUILT between 1775 and 1844, traditional textiles establish a look that is true to the house's heritage and true to the owner's taste for tailored elegance. As is appropriate to fine plantation homes of that period, the upholstery, curtains, and bed dressings feature such fancy fabrics as silk and toile, which are tucked, draped, and gathered into classic fabric treatments that deliberately underscore an early American sensibility.

Eighteenth-century designs from Colonial Williamsburg were the inspiration for the bed hangings in the master bedroom, where just one fabric — in a monochromatic red-and-white scheme

DRAPED IN LUXURIOUS
SWAGS, WINDOW AND
BED TREATMENTS IN
A MATCHING PRINT
RECALL TRADITIONAL
AMERICAN FABRIC
STYLING IN THIS
ELEGANT VIRGINIA
COUNTRY HOUSE.

reminiscent of toile — coordinates with the room's lacquerlike trim. Although each component of the bedclothes is relatively tailored, generous draping creates a luxurious effect. To enhance it, matching curtains were given more "volume" than is usual with deeper pleats and a fuller swag.

The living room incorporates dark-toned silks with understated patterns, which accentuate the formal style set by the furniture. Displaying a favored decorative motif of the early 1800s, the upholstery on the mahogany Empire sofa, for instance, is a deep royal blue highlighted with gold laurel wreaths. Similar in feeling is the chair upholstery, a burgundy silk that is patterned with small gold medallions. A variation on the print appears in the linings of the swag draperies, which have an elaborate design that also recalls window festoons seen at Colonial Williamsburg. ⌐×⊳

a light *touch*

in a Connecticut Greek Revival

COUNTERACTING THE AUSTERE LINES AND compact confines of a 1791 Greek Revival house in the Connecticut River Valley called for a gentle approach, with fabrics providing curvaceous shapes, compelling patterns, and summery colors. Using gracefully swagged curtains, pretty trims, and even fabric "upholstery" on walls and ceilings, designer Holly Holden was able to soften the hard edge of the architecture by shaping a gracious, feminine decor throughout.

Each room features one pronounced fabric element, subtly underscored by supporting players. In the living room, the focus is a needlepoint carpet

A SHIRRED WINDOW VALANCE,
PLEATED SLIPCOVERS, AND SUCH
COMFORTING ACCESSORIES AS A QUILT
AND THROW PILLOWS CREATE SOFT
LINES IN THE LIVING ROOM.

BELOW: A FEMININE GLAZED
CHINTZ PLAYS TRICKS WITH
SPACE IN THE MASTER BEDROOM.
THE GATHERED BED PELMET
APPEARS TO RAISE THE CEILING
LINE AND MAKE THE BED SEEM
LARGER, WHILE THE WINDOW
VALANCE AND CURTAINS
HELP MINIMIZE THE LONG,
NARROW SHAPE OF THE OPENING
BY GIVING IT EXTRA DIMENSION.
PALE PINK FABRIC COVERS BOTH
WALLS AND CEILING.

ABOVE AND OPPOSITE: FEATURING
A LARGE-SCALE SCENIC PATTERN
AND A SINGLE CLEAR COLOR ON AN
OFF-WHITE GROUND, WALL-TO-
WALL TOILE IS BOTH PRACTICAL AND
DECORATIVE IN THE DINING ROOM.
THE FABRIC HIDES BLEMISHES IN
THE UNDERLYING PLASTER AND
ALSO CREATES A STRIKING,
MURAL-LIKE BACKDROP. GATHERED
SWAG-AND-JABOT CURTAINS
IN THE WINDOWS PROVIDE JUST THE
RIGHT TOUCH OF SOFTNESS WITHOUT
OBSTRUCTING THE VIEW.

abloom with large-scale bouquets in roses, blues, and golds. The gold tone then repeats in the piping on tailored duck slipcovers, in the embroidered linen ottoman, and in the striped silk draperies.

The main theme in the dining room centers on the striking rose linen toile, which completely cocoons the room — upholstering walls, folding into gentle ripples at the windows, and even decking the lampshades. Elegant in their simplicity, ivory silk damask chair seats and cutwork linens are classic accompaniments. The rose palette carries into the master bedroom, there quieted to a dusky pink. In this room, fabric on the walls and ceiling not only establishes a soothing sense of enclosure but also acts as a foil for the delicate chintz draping the bed and window.

personal *style*

in a seasonal decor

LEAN, ELEGANT, AND IDIOSYNCRATIC IS THE trademark look of Beth Copeland Williams's apartment, where fabrics keep the decor fresh and flexible. Devising an eclectic interior, this Manhattan designer relied on classic prints and textures but shook up the mix in delightfully unexpected ways. Exotic leopard-print pillows nestle against humble ticking-stripe chair cushions; ottomans cased in velvety Oriental rug fragments stand on a breezy sisal rug; filmy silk curtains billow at windows; and paisley shawls pose as furniture throws.

Particularly innovative is the designer's use of slipcovers, which change the character of both the

Secured with jaunty bows, simple striped slipcovers used on Federal-style shield-back chairs bring a fresh, summery feel to the dark-paneled dining room.

furniture and the entire interior. In the dining room, for instance, where plywood paneling is faux painted in a rich cherry, slipcovers "deformalize" the look of classic furnishings. Here, casual striped back covers and skirted seats lighten up the stiff lines of reproduction 18th-century chairs.

The living room is the house chameleon. In cooler months, the room is swathed in fabrics, including slipcovers and throws on the seating pieces. In summer, however, the space is stripped of all its luxurious silk and velvet pillows, the Oriental rug, and the sofa throws to become a clean, cool space, perfect for warmer weather. ⌐⊶

LEFT: STRIPES, PLAIDS, AND SOLIDS MINGLE IN THE
LIVING ROOM, SOMETIMES WITH SURPRISING PRINTS.
THE RICH TEXTURES AND PATTERNS OF THE PAISLEY
THROWS, LEOPARD-PATTERN PILLOWS, AND CARPET-
COVERED OTTOMANS KEEP THE LOOK WARM IN WINTER.

ABOVE: THE UNSTRUCTURED DRAPE OF A
WOVEN THROW GIVES THIS CHAIR FLUID FORM.

vintage *collections*

in an 1840s country house

CLEVER DETAILS SET OFF SPARKS OF INTEREST IN
this New England retreat, where a variety of vintage
fabrics gathered over a lifetime imbues the home
with a casual, warm character. Cottons, silks, linens,
and laces that the homeowner has rescued over the
years from antique shops and family attics are
cleverly recycled, contributing inviting textures and
exquisitely muted colors to the lighthearted decor.

Here, improvisation is the guiding force. A
remnant of chintz might become "new" upholstery
for a chair, while elegant lingerie lace, scraps of
patterned silk saved from an old dress, swatches of
embroidery, lengths of fringe, and snippets of crochet

A UNIFYING
PALETTE OF QUIET
BLUES, PINKS, AND
GREENS IS CARRIED
THROUGH IN
PILLOWS AND
OTHER ACCESSORIES
IN THE BEDROOM.

BELOW: PILLOWS COVERED IN
19TH-CENTURY LACE-TRIMMED
LINEN, A PRETTY CHINTZ, SATIN
OVERLAID WITH LINGERIE
LACE, AND A HEAVY PATTERNED
SILK MAKE A FABRIC STILL LIFE
AGAINST A HEADBOARD
UPHOLSTERED IN SILK SHANTUNG.
SHINING THROUGH THE FABRIC
SHADE, SOFT LAMPLIGHT
CASTS BUTTERFLIES AND
FLOWERS — EMBROIDERED IN
THE 19TH CENTURY —
IN AN ETHEREAL GLOW.

turn up as eye-catching cases for throw and roll pillows. A fragment of 19th-century crewelwork has even been fashioned into a lampshade.

Joining the mix are several antique Oriental carpets, often overlapped to provide coordinating texture and pattern. Contemporary textiles also make an appearance — including a Portuguese needle-point rug with a loose, abstract design that complements the tighter, more naturalistic floral patterns of vintage upholstery and pillows in the bedroom. Yet despite this apparently carefree approach, the look never becomes too frivolous, because a single tenet of classic design prevails: no matter how the patterns may differ, they are always unified by a harmonizing color palette. ⌐⊶

ABOVE: THE ORIGINAL VELVET
UPHOLSTERY STILL COVERS THE 1918
CAMELBACK SOFA IN THE DAY ROOM; THE
FACT THAT IT IS ALLOWED TO SHOW ITS AGE
ONLY MAKES THIS PIECE OF FURNITURE
MORE APPROACHABLE. NEW PLAID SILK
COVERS THE BANQUETTE CUSHIONS.

RIGHT: PILLOWS ENCASED IN EARLY
19TH-CENTURY HAND-SCREENED
LINEN CONTRAST WITH FUZZY CHENILLE
UPHOLSTERY ON THE SOFA. A CIRCLE
OF BOLDLY PRINTED LINEN TRANSFORMS
AN ORDINARY TABLE BY BECOMING A
FULL-LENGTH SKIRT.

classic *fabrics*

ABOVE LEFT: TRAPUNTO IS A TYPE OF "WHITE WORK" THAT WAS ESPECIALLY IN VOGUE AMONG SOPHISTICATED AMERICAN LADIES OF THE FEDERAL ERA. ALWAYS MADE WITH A TOP SHEET OF FINE WHITE CLOTH SO THAT THE ELABORATE STITCHING WAS CLEARLY VISIBLE, TRAPUNTO QUILTS LIKE THIS 19TH-CENTURY EXAMPLE ALSO FEATURE RAISED DESIGNS STUFFED WITH COTTON.

LEFT: HOMESPUNS TYPICALLY FEATURED CHECKS AND PLAIDS BECAUSE SUCH PATTERNS WERE EASY TO WEAVE. SIMPLE PLAID COVERS WORK WELL WITH THESE HEAVILY TURNED STRAIGHT-BACK CHAIRS, USED TO FURNISH AN 18TH-CENTURY PARLOR.

FABRICS OF ALL KINDS COUNTED AMONG THE most valued, and valuable, possessions of Colonial Americans and were available in unexpected variety — from the silken alapeen once found on upholstery to the cotton wigan used for bed linens. While some of these fabrics once common to 18th- and early 19th-century homes have long since disappeared, a remarkable range of types and patterns has passed down through the generations. And thanks to their timeless good looks, their associations with period design, and their adaptability, they have become American classics.

At the simplest end of the spectrum are the striped or checked homespuns, generally woven in blue or brown on white, that were part of every household from earliest Colonial times. Initially made of linen, then increasingly of cotton after the late 1700s, such relatively coarse cloth often turned up in bedding (both as pillowcases and hangings) and was also used for upholstery and slipcovers.

Supplied primarily by European import until domestic manufacturing began in the mid-1700s, fabrics with fancy printed or woven patterns were highly desired for many types of furnishings. Among the most popular was chintz, an exquisitely printed cotton that originated in India some time before the 1600s and was particularly prized for its brilliant colors and complex patterns. More sophisticated were the large-scale monochrome prints known as toiles de Jouy, usually in red, blue, or black on a white cotton-linen ground, that were produced in France beginning in the mid-1700s.

Needlework was largely the pastime of ladies of leisure, and while many of the fine needle arts were exercised on clothing (petticoats might be trimmed with crewelwork, for instance), they were also

applied to home furnishings. The zigzag bargello stitch, for example, also known as flame stitch, was favored for upholstery and "tablecloaths." And quilting, which developed here in the late 1700s, was essential for bed coverings of all types. Such stitchwork was originally devised to hold a warm stuffing material in place between two sheets of fabric. More important, it added a decorative pattern to plain-colored cotton and linsey-woolsey spreads and complemented the intricate patterns of a patchwork or appliquéd quilt.

window *treatments*

ABOVE LEFT: EVEN AFTER TRAVERSE RODS WERE INTRODUCED IN THE LATE 1700S, TIE-BACKS OF ALL TYPES WERE STILL USED TO HOLD CURTAINS OPEN. BY THE EARLY 1800S, HARDWARE STYLES HAD BECOME ESPECIALLY ORNATE, EXEMPLIFIED BY THE GILDED LAUREL-WREATH RINGS USED TO CATCH THE BILLOWING DRAPERY AT THE 1812 WICKHAM HOUSE IN RICHMOND, VIRGINIA.

LEFT: RINGS AND PINCH PLEATS MAKE GENTLE GATHERS; HERE, THE TRADITIONAL TREATMENT SOFTENS THE LOOK OF FRENCH DOORS WITHOUT INTERFERING WITH THEIR FUNCTION.

OPPOSITE: SWAGS AND JABOTS DESCENDED FROM THE FESTOON CURTAINS POPULAR IN THE MID-1700S AND ARE THE PERFECT CHOICE TO BRING PERIOD FLAVOR TO A CONTEMPORARY COLONIAL-STYLE FARMHOUSE SUCH AS THIS.

BELOW: TYPICALLY RATHER FORMAL, THE CLASSIC SWAG TAKES ON A MORE RELAXED LOOK WHEN STYLED WITH A FLORAL-PRINT CHINTZ. THE JABOTS, OR TAILS, CAN BE DRAPED IN VARIOUS STYLES AND ACCENTED WITH CONTRASTING LININGS.

CURTAINS WERE LUXURIES IN EARLY COLONIAL times, found only in the homes of the well-to-do and generally only in the best rooms, such as the parlor and bed chamber, where they would be coordinated with upholstery and bed dressings. Plain green serge, a worsted woolen fabric, was considered the height of fashion around the late 1600s. But gradually in the 18th century, colorful calicos and linens began appearing, followed by fine wools and silks. Damask and satin, along with cheerful chintzes, became the curtain fabrics of choice for the more formal decor of the Federal period.

As the custom for draping windows became more widespread, a range of distinctive styles developed that remain familiar in American interiors today. The most elementary consisted of a piece of fabric hung straight from the top of the window to the sill — either suspended from a rod or fastened with tacks — and pulled to one side with a tie as needed. Not until the 18th century did it become more common to hang curtains as a pair; a valance might be used to hide the hardware.

Gathered curtain styles were much more fashionable throughout the late 18th and early 19th centuries. Among these were the festoon, a piece of fabric drawn up on cords at the corners to form a graceful swag. "Venetian" curtains were similar to modern Roman shades, in which the entire lower edge of the fabric fastens to a bar that is raised on hidden strings to form soft bunching at the window top. Tassels and decorative cords became an increasingly important part of the decor with these "moveable" curtains, and valances developed accordingly, often designed as elaborate cornices made of stiffened fabric or wood, perhaps decorated with paint or inlay.

LEFT: BALLOON SHADES, WHICH HAVE PUFFY GATHERS AND A CURVY SHAPE, TAKE THE LINEAR EDGE OFF A WINDOW IN A 1920S COUNTRY COTTAGE ON A NEW YORK LAKE.

BELOW: AN ASYMMETRICAL SWAG TREATMENT LENDS A CLASSIC BUT COMFORTABLE LOOK TO AN 1850S CONNECTICUT FARMHOUSE; THE TAIL IS CAUGHT IN A SOFT ROSETTE INSTEAD OF HANGING IN TAILORED PLEATS.

ABOVE: THE TRADITIONAL AMERICAN
CUSTOM OF COORDINATING CURTAINS WITH
OTHER FABRICS TAKES A TWIST IN
THIS KITCHEN, WHERE THE BOLD
UPHOLSTERY CHECK ALSO TRIMS NATURAL-
COLORED LINEN DRAPERIES.

ABOVE RIGHT: AN ELABORATION ON
THE SOFT FABRIC VALANCE, THE STIFFER
CORNICE HAS A STRONGLY SHAPED OUTLINE.

RIGHT: BY THE MID-19TH CENTURY,
WINDOW TREATMENTS HAD BECOME QUITE
ELABORATE. THE DINING ROOM OF
THIS 1850S TOWNHOUSE FEATURES SWAGS
WITH ASYMMETRICAL JABOTS AND
SHEER INNER CURTAINS HELD WITH
TASSELED CORDS. FRINGE ADDS YET
ANOTHER LAYER OF LUXURY.

upholstery

ABOVE LEFT: FURNITURE OF THE EMPIRE ERA,
IN THE EARLY 1800S, WAS OFTEN SO ORNATE
THAT THE UPHOLSTERY ITSELF WAS SUBDUED,
LEST IT COMPETE FOR ATTENTION.
CHARACTERISTIC OF THE PERIOD, THIS
SETTEE IS COVERED IN A SOLID FABRIC
TRIMMED WITH COORDINATING CORDING.

LEFT: WROUGHT IN WOOL YARNS
ON CANVAS, CREWELWORK, BARGELLO,
AND OTHER STITCHERY BEGAN APPEARING ON
COLONIAL AMERICAN CHAIRS AND SETTEES IN
THE EARLY 1700S, WHEN IT WAS OFTEN
RESERVED FOR THE MOST VISIBLE AREAS.
CONFINED TO THE INSIDE SURFACES, THE
ORIGINAL NEEDLEWORK UPHOLSTERY ON
THIS 18TH-CENTURY WING CHAIR SHOWS
A TYPICAL TREATMENT OF THE PERIOD.

OPPOSITE: FLORAL-PATTERNED FABRICS
HAVE BEEN A FAVORITE FOR UPHOLSTERY
IN AMERICA SINCE THE 1700S.
IN THIS LIVING ROOM, A CLASSIC FLORAL
CHINTZ HELPS UNIFY TWO ARMCHAIRS
AND AN OTTOMAN TO CREATE A COZY
SEATING AREA IN THE LARGE,
HIGH-CEILINGED SPACE.

BELOW: THE UPHOLSTERER'S ART
OFTEN ENTAILS THE MARRIAGE OF
FABRIC AND WOOD. ON THIS LOUIS XV ARM-
CHAIR, A PRETTY MIX OF INFORMAL PLAID
AND HIGH-STYLE DAMASK IN SOLID YELLOW
FOLLOWS PERFECTLY EVERY UNDULATION
OF THE SEAT AND BACK. BLUE PIPING ADDS
SUBTLE TAILORING.

INDISPENSABLE FOR COMFORT, THE TIGHTLY FITTED, permanent fabric covering that defines form and silhouette has evolved considerably from its beginnings. In 17th-century America, upholstery generally meant leather finished with ornamental brass tacks, since most fabric was considered far too precious and fragile to use for covering furniture. One of the only options available for bringing color and pattern to seating pieces was so-called Turkey work, a durable woolen pile fabric knotted to resemble the Turkish rugs that came to the Colonies around 1650.

As fabrics became more available in the 1700s, however, the art of upholstery began developing in America. Stuffings, including textile padding as well as grass and hay, added softness and shaping to the cushions, backs, and arms of seating pieces; cloth coverings enhanced the beauty of the wooden frame. The most commonly used types around the mid-18th century were worsted fabrics, often dyed in bright red, blue, or gold and stamped with a pattern that might imitate the wavy grain of more expensive silk moiré or the flat floral figuring of damask. Just as desirable — and popular — was "haircloth," in which long horse hairs were woven with wool or linen to create a fabric with the satiny finish and texture of silk damask; this, too, was dyed in bright colors and also in black.

By the late 1700s, however, an even greater range of upholstery fabrics had become available, with choice silks, satins, velvets, and chintzes preferred for the finest furniture pieces. Today the selection is virtually limitless, ranging from canvas ducks to sturdy quilted fabrics that wear well. Solid colors and small prints work particularly well with complex furniture shapes and are always at home in a classic scheme. ←

Elements of design
slipcovers

ABOVE LEFT: WITH THEIR SOFT, LOOSE
DRAPE, SLIPCOVERS TEND TO LOOK MORE
CASUAL THAN UPHOLSTERY; THE SOFA COVER
IN THIS STUDY PROVIDES THE PERFECT
COUNTERPOINT TO THE FORMAL LINES
OF THE STRONGLY GEOMETRIC WALLPAPER.

LEFT: "FURNITURE CHECK,"
GENERALLY ANY FABRIC WITH A BOLDER,
LARGER CHECK PATTERN, WAS A POPULAR
CHOICE FOR COLONIAL SLIPCOVERS IN
AMERICA. BOW TIES ON THIS UPDATED
CHAIR COVER ADD A NOTE OF WHIMSY
TO A TRADITIONAL STYLE.

SINCE FINE UPHOLSTERY FABRICS WERE SO expensive and valuable, Colonial householders of all stations naturally wanted to protect their investments: from wear, insect damage, spills, fading, and a host of other perils. Introduced as early as the 18th century, the solution was slipcovers. Also called "cases," slipcovers not only afforded protection but also offered numerous other benefits that made the covers as functional two hundred years ago as they are now.

Often made of a cool, lightweight fabric such as cotton muslin or linen holland, slipcovers helped make upholstery — especially scratchy wool and horsehair and other heavy fabrics that did not "breathe" — more comfortable to sit on in hot summer months. For this reason, they were especially popular in the South. The covers also allowed homeowners to vary the look of a room at less cost than with new upholstery. Should a chair or sofa covering be worn beyond repair, it could be hidden handily beneath a removable cover. And when the dark velvets and wools that seemed so cozy in winter began to look uninviting as warm weather approached, covers in a light-colored, lightweight fabric could make a room appear fresh and breezy.

One further advantage was that slipcovers could be removed easily for laundering. Even if they could not always be pressed crisply into shape, their slightly rumpled look only added to the casual charm that makes these versatile classics so appealing to this day. ☙

Elements of design
the well-made bed

ABOVE LEFT: APPLIQUÉD QUILTS DISPLAY THE TYPICALLY ELABORATE PATTERNS AMERICAN WOMEN ACHIEVED JUST BY STITCHING FABRIC CUT-OUTS TO A PLAIN BACKGROUND.

ABOVE: THIS CIRCA-1740 BED "RUGG" FROM MAINE FEATURES THE OVERALL FLORAL PATTERN TYPICAL OF SUCH COVERS, FOUND PRIMARILY IN NEW ENGLAND.

LEFT: THE MASTER BEDROOM OF THE 1818 FÉLIX VALLÉ HOUSE IN MISSOURI CONTAINS A MAHOGANY TESTER BED DRESSED WITH A GLAZED COTTON QUILT; THE BED IN THE ADJOINING CHILD'S ROOM HAS A SIMPLER WOOLEN COVERLET. SUCH WOVEN SPREADS WERE MADE BOTH ON HOME LOOMS AND BY PROFESSIONALS FROM THE MID-1700S THROUGH THE 1800S.

By far the most precious of Colonial textiles were those used on the bed. Indeed, beyond their practical purpose of providing sleepers with warmth and privacy, a full set of "bed furniture" (including at least a coverlet, a tester, and curtains that completely enclosed the bed) was a coveted status symbol, as well as an artistic outlet for the women who stitched them.

The most basic bed coverings were made from plain woven fabrics, such as homespuns, although silks, velvets, and wools were found in the bed chambers of the wealthy. By the mid-18th century, it was also possible, and fashionable, to dress the bed with colorfully patterned fabrics, including chintz, calico, and copperplate-printed cottons.

Bedclothes featuring decorative needle arts were also prized. Among the earliest types, made in the 1700s, was the bed "rugg," a plush spread of woolen yarns looped through a wool or linen background. Also favored at the time were crewelwork bed furnishings, often expertly embroidered with naturalistic motifs. Perhaps the best-known stitched bed textile is the quilt. Beginning around the early 1800s, American women developed quilting beyond utility and thrift into a folk-art form, creating graphic patterns and innovative designs that set these bedcovers apart from all others. ←

ABOVE: CURTAINS GATHERED UP WITH CORDS ENCLOSE A FEDERAL-ERA BED.

LEFT: WHILE IT WAS CONSIDERED STYLISH IN THE 1700S AND 1800S FOR ALL BED FURNISHINGS TO MATCH, MANY FAMILIES SIMPLY DRESSED THE BEDS WITH WHATEVER FABRICS WERE AT HAND; THIS APPROACH CREATES A COZY LOOK.

Left: A monochromatic print provides the right touch for the period and relaxed style of this guest room in a 1775 cottage in New York's rustic Taconic Hills.

Below: The mid-18th-century bed "furniture" stitched by Mary Bulman of Maine comprises three valances, four curtains, a headcloth, and a shaped spread. The only complete set of crewelwork bedclothes in existence from 18th-century America, the textiles are remarkable for their graceful motifs and superb stitchery.

Opposite: Fabric works magic in this Manhattan apartment bedroom, turning a relatively plain four-poster into a more prominent element. A canopy frame and curtain rods suspended from the ceiling are fitted with a pleated valance and draperies sweeping the floor. Balancing the pronounced chinoiserie motif is a plain white coverlet with a scalloped edge that picks up the deep red tone from the printed pattern.

CHAPTER FOUR If architecture forms the bones of a room, then furniture is the muscle — filling out the frame, lending heft and definition, and providing a sense of balance, flexibility, and motion. Even when all the other decorative touches are in place, a room without furniture falls flat.

The primary function of furniture is, of course, to satisfy certain basic needs: a chair for sitting, a chest for storing. Yet needs change with time and cultural customs, as do interpretations of how best to meet them. This has resulted in an array of furniture designs, from sophisticated "high" styles to rustic "low" ones, that today allows for considerable latitude in creating a desired look.

Consider the Queen Anne tea table. Introduced in the early 18th century, this graceful form was conceived as a convenient stand on which to serve a drink newly fashionable in the West. But it had another function: to indicate that the owner had sufficient income for a luxury and the leisure time to indulge in a refined social ritual. Tea is no longer a status symbol, but the Queen Anne tea table is still

furniture

serviceable. Why? Because superior workmanship, beautiful materials, and classic lines help it to perform beyond its original narrow purpose.

Today that same table — or a Chippendale chair, an Empire sofa, or any other example of fine design — can fit as comfortably into a contemporary house as it can into a Georgian manse of the 1730s. It can quietly take its place in a room full of its fellows, contributing to a unified, traditional decor. And it can also act as a stunning counterpoint to the informal charm of whimsically painted country pieces or create a classic accent among comfortably plump chairs and sofas that suit the taste for overstuffed upholstered pieces.

Comfort, of course, is the ultimate goal. The finest collection of antiques will not improve a decor if an interior ends up looking like a museum display. To keep rooms welcoming, consider cozy fireside groupings, intimate dining arrangements, or a chair placed to take advantage of a view. Furniture should not just invite people into a room; it should make them want to stay.

classic & contemporary

in a five-room flat

New and old, shy and bold, formal and free-spirited — all come together in this New York apartment to create a welcoming atmosphere. It's a faultless balancing act, whereby the desire to display the fruits of a lifelong passion for collecting is well weighed against the need for practicality and comfort.

The core of the furnishings is a highly eclectic assembly of classics in which no one period, style, or country of origin predominates. Everything from a regal Empire-style reclining couch to workaday Windsor chairs mingles in carefree combinations. English Queen Anne chairs surround an American Chippendale dining table — all overseen by an early

RIGHT: HIGH STYLE MEETS FOLK ART IN THE MASTER BEDROOM, WHERE TWO PIECES OF EARLY 19TH-CENTURY FURNITURE BALANCE EACH OTHER WITH DIFFERENT MOODS. THE SHERATON HIGH-POST BED REFLECTS FEDERAL-ERA FORMALITY, IN WHICH REEDING AND CLASSICAL ORNAMENTS, SUCH AS THE URN FINIALS, WERE CONSIDERED VERY CHIC. BY CONTRAST, THE 1810 STRAIGHT-FRONT CHEST OF DRAWERS IS A COUNTRY PIECE, DECORATED WITH GRAIN PAINTING MEANT TO IMITATE THE HIGHLY FIGURED WOODS THEN USED AS VENEERS.

LEFT: ALTHOUGH THE OVERALL FEEL OF THE INTERIORS IS CASUAL, A FEW FORMAL FURNISHINGS PROVIDE STRONG ACCENTS. THIS EARLY 19TH-CENTURY EMPIRE RECAMIER WITH A FIGURED MAHOGANY FRAME AND MOHAIR CUSHIONS PIPED IN NATURAL ROPE, SERVES AS A COUNTERPOINT TO THE MORE UNDERSTATED CONTEMPORARY UPHOLSTERED PIECES. ITS BIG PERSONALITY ALSO PLAYS AGAINST THE SIMPLE GEORGIAN LINES OF THE LATE 18TH-CENTURY TILT-TOP TRIPOD TABLE AT ITS FOOT.

1800s Swedish tall-case clock — while a folksy faux-painted chest shows up next to a high-style Federal-era bed.

Offsetting the strong lines of the high-profile antiques are "sink-in" soft upholstered pieces. To help highlight the antiques and prevent the mix from becoming overwhelming, these contemporary furnishings keep a low profile — literally. "Not everything has to be precious," explains the designer, Eric Cohler. "Some pieces need to be foils." Thus, he purposely chose tight-back sofas and club chairs with broad proportions, simple roll arms, and tailored coverings that do not draw attention to themselves. Squat ottomans take the place of coffee tables, further enhancing a soft look.

LEFT: THE RELATIVELY PLAIN LINES OF THE 1770 DINING TABLE ARE A FOIL FOR EXQUISITE JAPANNED QUEEN ANNE CHAIRS, EACH BEARING A DIFFERENT SCENE PAINTED IN ORIENTAL STYLE ON THE VASE SPLAT.

ABOVE: THE QUINTESSENTIAL CHAMELEON CHAIR IS THE WINDSOR, WHOSE SIMPLE, STRAIGHTFORWARD DESIGN FITS IN ANYWHERE. IN THE BREAKFAST ROOM, A VARIETY OF 19TH-CENTURY SACK-BACKS TEAMS UP WITH A STURDY OAK TABLE FROM A GRAND OLD LONG ISLAND RESORT HOTEL.

an *American collection*

in a Connecticut River hideaway

THE HOUSE MAY BE COLONIAL REVIVAL, BUILT IN the 1940s, but the furniture it contains is authentic: a superb collection of high-style American antiques from the 18th and early 19th centuries gathered by three generations of connoisseurs. Against walls paneled in cypress and chestnut shine fine examples of cabinetmaking from the Queen Anne, Chippendale, and Federal periods, a number of which were crafted in the country's foremost urban furniture shops.

Here, the furniture makes for a formal look, as polished brass hardware and dark, fine-grained woods like mahogany, walnut, and maple lend a dignified presence. Fabrics also contribute to the

EXCEPTIONAL
ANTIQUES
INCLUDE A DROP-
LEAF TABLE BY
DUNCAN PHYFE
AND A TRIPOD
STAND BY
CHARLES-HONORÉ
LANNUIER.

subdued elegance, as exemplified by the matched pair of square-back Federal sofas covered in silk. Many pieces are also subtly and exquisitely decorated: such details as the carved acanthus leaf on a table leg or the intricate wood inlay of a sideboard demonstrate how craftsmanship can underscore an overall effect.

Yet despite the high quality of the antiques, these rooms never look unapproachable. One reason is the relative simplicity of American pieces. While English furniture of the same period is very elaborate, says the collector, American examples are more refined and restrained — and here contribute to the approachable and lived-in look of the house itself. ☞

ABOVE: DAINTY TRIFID FEET ON A WALNUT CHAIR FROM PHILADELPHIA AND A CRISP SHELL CARVING ON A CHERRY LOWBOY FROM NEW HAVEN, CONNECTICUT, EXEMPLIFY THE ESPECIALLY ELEGANT DETAIL OF TWO QUEEN ANNE PIECES.

RIGHT: BESIDE A 1790S HEPPLEWHITE SIDEBOARD IS A SIDE CHAIR WITH A SPLAT CARVED IN THE SO-CALLED PRINCE OF WALES FEATHERS MOTIF. THIS SPLAT FORM, WHICH APPEARED IN THE 1793 EDITION OF THOMAS SHERATON'S BOOK OF FURNITURE DESIGNS, WAS POPULAR AMONG NEW YORK CRAFTSMEN.

LEFT: THE MAHOGANY CHIPPENDALE CHEST IN THE FRONT HALL WAS CRAFTED IN MASSACHUSETTS AROUND 1770 AND REPRESENTS THE LEVEL OF SOPHISTICATION THAT MASTER CABINETMAKERS IN BOSTON, NEWPORT, RHODE ISLAND, AND OTHER NEW ENGLAND TRADE CENTERS ACHIEVED. THE DEMANDING DESIGN CALLED FOR DRAWERS WITH SQUARED ENDS AND A SHALLOW SERPENTINE CURVE IN THE CENTER; EACH FRONT IS CARVED FROM A SINGLE THICK BOARD. THE ORNATE BRASS WILLOW MOUNTS AND ESCUTCHEONS FURTHER CONTRIBUTE TO THE PIECE'S FORMAL STYLE.

RIGHT: THE RESTRAINED STYLE OF A FLAT-TOP MAHOGANY CHIPPENDALE HIGHBOY FROM NEW YORK IS COMPATIBLE WITH THE GRACEFUL LINES OF A NEOCLASSICAL CANOPIED FIELD BED IN MAPLE. THE ADJACENT SIDE CHAIR IS A GOOD EXAMPLE OF THE CONSERVATIVE TASTE IN THE NORTHEASTERN COLONIES. MADE IN NEWPORT AROUND 1770, IT FEATURES NONE OF THE FLAMBOYANT CARVING OFTEN ASSOCIATED WITH CHAIRS OF THE PERIOD. INSTEAD, THE BACK SPLAT COMPRISES ELEGANTLY INTERTWINED LINES, WHICH FLOW INTO A LIGHTLY CURVED CREST WITH DELICATELY CARVED, UPTURNED CORNERS, OR "EARS."

Colonial *furnishings*

in a reproduction farmstead

EARLY AMERICAN ANTIQUES TURN BACK TIME AND complete the illusion set by the architecture of this Virginia home, which was built only three decades ago in the style of an 18th-century New England farmhouse. Such Colonial-era touches as paneled walls and brick floors provide the perfect backdrop for furniture that would have been found in a prosperous period home on the eastern seaboard.

As was often customary in the 1700s, the "fanciest" examples furnish the parlor. Large, imposing pieces in the ornate William and Mary style, such as a highboy poised on trumpet-shaped legs and a leather-covered side chair with an

A YELLOW-PINE DISH DRESSER, PROBABLY MADE IN VIRGINIA AROUND 1750, IS THE DRAMATIC CENTERPIECE OF THE DINING ROOM.

ABOVE: A WILLIAM AND MARY TRUMPET-LEG
HIGHBOY, BANNISTER-BACK CHAIR, GATELEG
TABLE, AND LEATHER-UPHOLSTERED CHAIR
WITH CARVED CREST BRING A UNIFIED LOOK
TO THE PARLOR. THE BUN FOOT SEEN ON
THE HIGHBOY WAS A PREVALENT
FEATURE OF THE PERIOD.

LEFT: THE MASTER BEDROOM FEATURES A
MIX OF COUNTRY PIECES, INCLUDING A
QUEEN ANNE TABLE, CHIPPENDALE
CHEST OF DRAWERS, AND FEDERAL
HANGING CUPBOARD. THE
MID-18TH-CENTURY PENCIL-POST BED WAS
MADE IN NEW ENGLAND OF HIGHLY
GRAINED TIGER MAPLE.

intricately carved crest, bring a pleasing sense of grandeur to the otherwise simple living room.

In the rest of the interior, country furniture in a variety of styles is mixed — much in the same manner as two centuries ago, when families held on to old pieces even as they acquired new ones. In a casual sitting room, for example, early 19th-century Windsor chairs gather around a maple tea table dated a century earlier. While relatively subtle, such small items as hanging cupboards and mirrors with decorative frames have strong impact and provide insight into the kind of incidental furnishings that also took pride of place in early American rooms.

BELOW: COUNTRY PIECES, INCLUDING WINDSOR CHAIRS AND A TEA TABLE, FURNISH THE SITTING ROOM. THE RAT-TAIL HANGING CUPBOARD IS TYPICAL OF THE SPACE-SAVING STORAGE PIECES USED IN 18TH-CENTURY HOMES. THE COURTING MIRROR ABOVE THE PENNSYLVANIA WALNUT DESK IS A TYPE OF LOVE TOKEN BROUGHT TO THE COLONIES IN THE EARLY 1700S FROM NORTHERN EUROPE.

sophisticated
country style
in a remodeled cabin

STARK SIMPLICITY LEAVENED WITH TOUCHES OF whimsy marks the interior decor of this 18th-century log house in Maryland, which was rebuilt as an informal gallery for antique American country furniture. Here, the room settings themselves are played down to let the contents come to the fore. Rather than wall and window treatments, it is the undulating tabletops, time-worn chair seats, and painted birds flitting on drawer fronts that bring the spare spaces to life.

The furniture's obvious and sometimes quirky handcraftsmanship is in perfect harmony with the hewn beams and fieldstone fireplace of the house. It also works well with the unstructured forms and

SET OFF BY SIMPLIFIED
SURROUNDINGS, 18TH-CENTURY
COUNTRY FURNISHINGS, INCLUDING
THE RUSH-SEATED LADDER-BACK
CHAIR AND WALNUT TRESTLE TABLE,
BECOME HIGHLIGHTS OF THE DECOR.

nubby upholstery of the new furniture, which blends quietly into the background.

What remains to be seen are the clean silhouettes and strong colors of country antiques as individual and vital as the hands that fashioned them. Each piece stands as a sculpture in itself, offering a detail or form that holds and delights the eye: a pattern of curvaceous chair slats, bench legs that bulge with chubby calves, or a chest's bulbous turnip feet that seem to poise on their toes. Natural tones of wood mellowed with age add warmth and also contrast with the paintwork. Some pieces are covered in one of the deep hues favored by rural craftsmen, and others bear the fanciful motifs that elevate a utilitarian object to a work of folk art. ⌒➤

OPPOSITE: A CIRCA-1740 WALNUT GATELEG TABLE FROM NEW ENGLAND IS SURROUNDED BY A MIXED ASSEMBLY OF BLACK-PAINTED WINDSOR CHAIRS — A BOW-BACK, A HOOP-BACK, AND A COMB-BACK — EACH AS INDIVIDUAL AS A DINNER GUEST. MADE IN MASSACHUSETTS IN THE EARLY 1700S, THE CHEST OF DRAWERS IS ELABORATELY PAINTED IN IMITATION OF THE JAPANNING TECHNIQUE USED ON HIGH-STYLE FURNITURE OF THE PERIOD — A COUNTRY PIECE WITH FANCY ASPIRATIONS.

LEFT: RECAST AS A SIDE TABLE FOR A PAIR OF SUITABLY UNDERSTATED ARMCHAIRS, A LATE 18TH-CENTURY PAINTED BLANKET CHEST DISPLAYS THE EYE-CATCHING HANDIWORK OF A VIRGINIA CRAFTSMAN.

Elements of design
classic styles

RIGHT AND BELOW RIGHT: THE SINUOUS CURVES OF THE QUEEN ANNE STYLE ARE SEEN IN THE FLOWING CABRIOLE LEG OF A HIGHBOY, THE SLENDER VASE SPLATS OF SIDE CHAIRS, AND THE DAINTY KNEES OF A TRIPOD STAND.

BELOW: FURNITURE IN THE WILLIAM AND MARY STYLE WAS MASSIVE AND HEAVY ENOUGH TO ADD PRESENCE TO LARGE, OFTEN DARK ROOMS. THIS EARLY 1700S DROP-LEAF BUTTERFLY TABLE, SO CALLED FOR THE WINGLIKE SUPPORTS, IS MATED WITH BANNISTER-BACK CHAIRS. SUCH SEATING PIECES OFTEN FEATURE ORNATE CRESTS, RING-TURNED LEGS, AND PAINTED FINISHES.

EARLY AMERICAN FURNITURE IS A BRILLIANT amalgam in which aspirations to gracious living blended with basic, practical needs, and notions of beauty were tempered by the materials and artisans at hand. The singular furniture that resulted reflects a certain dynamic spirit lasting well beyond the periods when it was considered the "newest manner." Certainly the styles prevailing from the 1600s to the early 1800s were influenced by those in Europe, primarily in England. However, American pieces were simpler overall and took on their own character as plentiful native woods replaced European species and patriotic symbols, such as the eagle, were mixed with traditional ornaments like urns and swags. From the Colonial to the post-Revolutionary periods, five major styles dominated in America, lagging some years behind European fashions.

Each is unmistakable in its individual hallmarks — often found in a foot, pediment, crest, or leg. The earliest style is William and Mary (popular in the Colonies roughly from 1690 to 1725), which derived from the heavy furniture in favor during the joint reign of England's William III and Mary II. Characteristic pieces such as bannister-back chairs and gateleg tables display the straight silhouettes, deep carvings and turnings, and dark finishes of the period.

The Queen Anne style (1725–50), named for that English monarch, is more restrained and human in scale. The accent is on symmetrical lines, elegant proportions, graceful curves, and polished woods — exemplified by the many tea tables of the era, with their cabriole legs and dainty pad feet.

Furniture of the Chippendale period (1750–80) again becomes ornate. Its English namesake, Thomas Chippendale, compiled the first British book of furniture design (*The Gentleman and Cabinetmaker's Director*) in 1754 and promoted a florid style with intricate lines, exaggerated curves, and rich carving. Bonnet-top highboys and pierced-splat chairs with ball-and-claw feet are prominent.

Federal furniture (1780–1815) is noted for refined lines, delicate shapes, and Neoclassical ornament, such as urns, often wrought in inlay or light carving. Typical pieces include square-back sofas and sideboards, with tapered legs ending in spade feet. George Hepplewhite and Thomas Sheraton are the two English designers who helped define this look.

Finally, the Empire style (1815–35) reflects tastes under French Emperor Napoleon I and takes Neoclassical furniture design to an extreme. Silhouettes, decoration, and finishes all become bolder and more pronounced, as is evident in the lyre motifs, paw feet, and gilded ornament that were the fashion.

ABOVE: THIS 1820S MAHOGANY TESTER BED, AFTER A DESIGN BY THOMAS SHERATON, EXEMPLIFIES THE PARED-DOWN FEDERAL STYLE. THE LEGS TAPER TO PLAIN CYLINDRICAL FEET, AND THE POSTS ARE LARGELY UNDECORATED EXCEPT FOR THE ELEGANT REEDING, A HALLMARK ORNAMENT OF EARLY 19TH-CENTURY FURNITURE. BEDS WITH CURVED TESTERS, OFTEN CALLED FIELD BEDS, CAME INTO FASHION EARLY IN THE FEDERAL PERIOD.

RIGHT: EMPIRE IS AMERICAN FURNITURE AT ITS MOST EXTRAVAGANT. THE FORMS BECOME VERY ELABORATE AND MAY BE DEEPLY CARVED; THIS LYRE-BACK CHAIR AND PAIR OF GRECIAN SOFAS ARE GOOD EXAMPLES. OFTEN GILDED FOR EMPHASIS, CLASSICAL DECORATIVE DEVICES LIKE THE LION'S-PAW FEET AND WINGED CARYATID FIGURE ADORNING THE SOFA TABLE WERE ALSO PROMINENT. NOT ONLY WERE THE GRIFFINS SUPPORTING THE PIER TABLE CLASSICAL MOTIFS, BUT THEIR EAGLE HEADS SERVED AS AN AMERICAN SYMBOL OF PATRIOTISM.

LEFT: WITH ITS LIGHT, DELICATE APPEARANCE AND UNMISTAKABLE BACK, THE HEART-SHAPED OR SHIELD-BACK CHAIR IS THE FURNITURE FORM PERHAPS MOST CLOSELY IDENTIFIED WITH THE FEDERAL STYLE. SUCH CHAIRS, WHICH WERE SHOWN IN GEORGE HEPPLEWHITE'S INFLUENTIAL 1788 BOOK, *CABINET-MAKER AND UPHOLSTERER'S GUIDE*, WERE OFTEN CONSTRUCTED OF MAHOGANY AND TYPICALLY FEATURE STRAIGHT, TAPERED LEGS AND STRAIGHT-SIDED SEATS. BESIDES THE CARVING ON THE BACKS, THEY MIGHT BE DECORATED WITH INLAY, ALSO SEEN HERE ON THE PERIOD GAMING TABLE.

Elements of design

country *furniture*

ABOVE LEFT: THE SPINDLE-BACK CHAIRS KNOWN AS WINDSORS WERE ONE OF THE MOST POPULAR COUNTRY FURNITURE FORMS FROM THE MID-1700S TO MID-1800S. THE FAN-BACK AND HOOP-BACK ARE BUT TWO OF THE MANY VARIATIONS.

ABOVE: ELEMENTARY SHAPES AND MINIMAL DECORATION CHARACTERIZE THE COUNTRY PIECES USED TO FURNISH THIS LIVING ROOM. DEVOID OF CARVING, THE MID-1700S PENNSYLVANIA SECRETARY IS A SIMPLIFIED VERSION OF THE MORE ELABORATE HIGH-STYLE PIECES OF THE ERA.

LEFT: THE SETTLE BENCH IS A MEDIEVAL FORM THAT ENDURED IN RURAL AMERICA INTO THE 1800S AND WAS TYPICALLY USED BY THE HEARTH. THIS EARLY EXAMPLE IS DISTINGUISHED BY ITS UNUSUALLY TALL, CURVED BACK, INTENDED TO SHELTER SITTERS FROM DRAFTS AND CONTAIN THE HEAT FROM THE FIRE.

BELOW: COUNTRY CRAFTSMEN SERVED A
CLIENTELE AS CONSERVATIVE AS THEMSELVES
AND OFTEN INCORPORATED OLDER,
OUTDATED ELEMENTS WHEN WORKING IN A
NEW STYLE. THE CHAIRS AROUND THIS
STRETCHER-BASE TABLE FEATURE THE VASE
SPLAT AND YOKE CREST RAIL
CHARACTERISTIC OF THE QUEEN ANNE STYLE,
ALBEIT IN SIMPLIFIED FORM; THE BULBOUS
TURNINGS ARE HOLDOVERS FROM THE
PRECEDING WILLIAM AND MARY PERIOD.

BELOW RIGHT: HINGED DROP-LEAF TABLES
LIKE THIS 18TH-CENTURY RED-PAINTED PIECE
FROM PENNSYLVANIA WERE FAVORITE COUNTRY
DESIGNS BECAUSE THEY SAVED SPACE,
AN ASSET IN CRAMPED LIVING QUARTERS.

As in the children's game of "telephone," in which a message becomes distorted as it passes from one person to another, American country furniture is an expression so removed from its origins that it has assumed a tone all its own. A distant echo of high fashion, this is furniture of the people: pragmatic, refreshingly unpretentious, often quirky pieces made by rural homeowners and joiners trying to imitate the sophisticated designs of urban master cabinetmakers, who in turn were adapting European fashions for their own clientele. Country pieces are instantly recognizable by their simplified lines and relaxed look. The silhouettes are usually devoid of the fussy frills that can mark high-style pieces, and the decoration is limited to paint, light carving, and inlay.

This is not to say that this furniture is plain or unimaginative. On the contrary, country artisans, working alone outside the mainstream, lent their pieces great individuality. The curve of a chair leg might be exaggerated simply to suit the maker's whim, or a chest might be carved with a special motif to satisfy a customer. Also, country craftsmen often had to compensate for lack of materials or skills, creating one-of-a-kind pieces with a make-do appearance or unconventional construction that only contributes to their allure.

Elements of design
painted *furniture*

ABOVE LEFT: AMONG THE MOST FAMILIAR AMERICAN PAINTED FURNITURE STYLES IS THE HITCHCOCK, A NAME REFERRING BOTH TO THE "FANCY" CHAIRS THAT CONNECTICUT TINKERER LAMBERT HITCHCOCK INTRODUCED IN 1818 AND TO THE COUNTLESS IMITATIONS THAT FOLLOWED. THESE TRUE HITCHCOCKS, FROM THE 1830S, FEATURE THE DISTINCTIVE GLOSSY PAINT FINISH DECORATED WITH GILTLIKE STENCILING, AS WELL AS ERGONOMIC SLATS AND SEATS.

ABOVE: JAPANNED FURNITURE WAS POPULAR IN AMERICA FROM THE EARLY 1700S TO THE EARLY 1800S; THE EXTREMELY ORNATE PAINTWORK ON THIS TRUMPET-LEGGED HIGHBOY WAS MEANT TO IMITATE ORIENTAL LACQUER.

LEFT: STROKES OF FAUX GRAINING DECORATE THIS SIMPLE COUNTRY BLANKET CHEST.

APPLIED TO ALL TYPES AND STYLES OF PIECES between the 1600s and early 1800s, paint was an essential element of furniture making that could work wonders by protecting bare wood, hiding flaws, prettifying a plain piece, or highlighting the fine details of elaborate examples. One of its most pervasive uses was to imitate the effects of other materials and ornamentation. Should precious woods and precision tools be lacking for veneer, faux painting could substitute for a figured grain. If gilding was the rage, a dab of gold or yellow paint provided a hint of glimmer at less cost. And when exotic lacquered furniture from Asia captured the imagination, American furniture makers employed the paint technique of japanning to simulate rare Oriental lacquerwork.

Paint was also an effective cover-up, concealing soft or inferior hardwoods that had little decorative value. A coat of paint could disguise clashing hues and grains when different woods were combined in one piece. Windsor chairs were nearly always painted, for example, because their construction required both pliable and sturdy types of wood that appeared mismatched if left exposed. Finally, when it came to calling attention to a piece, little surpassed paint. Outlined in a contrasting color, a turned leg, carved crest, or raised panel was suddenly more prominent. Even flat surfaces gained dimension and interest when flower bouquets sprouted on tabletops or whimsical angels hovered on drawer fronts.

LEFT: DECORATION BECAME INCREASINGLY BOLD IN THE EARLY 19TH CENTURY, HAND IN HAND WITH THE HEAVIER FURNITURE FORMS OF THE DAY. THE FLAMBOYANT PATTERN ON THIS COUNTRY EMPIRE CHEST SUGGESTS THE WAVY GRAIN OF THE TIGER MAPLE IN FAVOR AT THE TIME.

ABOVE: GERMANIC SETTLERS IN PENNSYLVANIA WERE AMONG THE MOST ENTHUSIASTIC PRACTITIONERS OF PAINTED DECORATION. THIS BRACKET-FOOT CHEST, ORNAMENTED WITH TULIP MOTIFS, IS TYPICAL OF THEIR TRADITIONAL DOWER CHESTS OF THE 1700S, IN WHICH YOUNG WOMEN STORED ITEMS IN ANTICIPATION OF MARRIAGE.

RIGHT: BROAD CHAIR BACKS AND SPLATS WERE IDEAL SURFACES FOR DECORATION. THESE EARLY 19TH-CENTURY CHAIRS BOAST THE ACANTHUS LEAF AND GREEK KEY DESIGNS THEN IN VOGUE.

Elements of design
antiques &
reproductions

ABOVE LEFT: THESE REPRODUCTIONS FEATURE
PERIOD HARDWARE AND FINE MATERIALS,
INCLUDING THE SAME VENEERS AND EXOTIC
WOODS HIGHLY PRIZED IN THE FEDERAL ERA.
THIS PIECE RE-CREATES THE DESIGN OF A
CHEST FROM PORTSMOUTH,
NEW HAMPSHIRE, AND IS CRAFTED OF
MAHOGANY AND TIGER MAPLE.

ABOVE: A CIRCA-1750 MAINE HIGHBOY
PAINTED WITH BLACK FEATHERLIKE MOTIFS ON
AN OCHER GROUND (TO SUGGEST COSTLY BURL)
INSPIRED THIS REPRODUCTION,
ALSO FAUX-FINISHED BY HAND.

LEFT: REPRODUCTIONS MIX COMFORTABLY
AND OFTEN IMPERCEPTIBLY WITH ORIGINALS.
IN THIS LIVING ROOM, A CONTEMPORARY WING
CHAIR WITH CREWELWORK UPHOLSTERY HOLDS
ITS OWN WITH A 1790s HEPPLEWHITE
EXAMPLE OF THE SAME FORM.

ANTIQUE FURNITURE IS A TREASURE, A TANGIBLE link to the country's heritage of handcraftsmanship that also offers sheer visual delight with its timeless designs and fine finishes mellowed by age. While there can be great pride and pleasure in owning the real thing, reproductions also have their place. Like antiques themselves, they are available in a range of styles and prices and can display an equally high level of decoration and detail, down to the inlay and hardware.

Furniture designs have been adapted and reproduced for centuries. Some of the earliest, mid-17th-century Colonial styles, for example, were derived from medieval European pieces. Beginning around the mid-19th century, numerous furniture types from the past were resurrected and reproduced, the best-known example being the Colonial Revival style inspired by the 1876 Centennial Exhibition in Philadelphia.

The appeal of reproduction furniture was the same then as it is now. When an antique is unavailable or unaffordable, a well-constructed, historically faithful copy can provide a comparable look, generally at lesser cost. Reproductions may also hold up better under heavy use: although handcraftsmanship was meant to last, some antiques become fragile over time, making new furniture a practical choice.

Traditional designs in new furniture can also be adapted to fill contemporary tastes and needs. A blanket chest, for example, might be enlarged in scale to sit comfortably at the end of a king-size bed. And, of course, classic designs adapt well to later forms that simply did not exist in the Colonial era, such as the coffee table. ←

CHAPTER FIVE Endowing a room with warmth, character, and decorative highlights, accessories are the final strokes of any good design scheme. These small but effective details can elevate an already interesting interior into a truly impressive one or add polish to a lackluster space so it dazzles.

How to add the right finishing touches? There are no hard-and-fast rules for accessorizing because choosing decorative accents, which might be anything from a bouquet of wildflowers to a set of Staffordshire assembled over a lifetime, is largely a matter of following instinct. If an object or arrangement is beautiful to your own eye, chances are you will never tire of it. And that means it will be a timeless addition to your home.

Yet classic accessories do more than just look pretty. They demonstrate an attention to detail, indicating that extra effort was expended to make a room even more pleasing and comfortable. They also add interest and diversity: their smaller scale plays off the proportions of large pieces of furniture, and they can be used to introduce splashes of

finishing *touches*

contrasting color, pattern, or texture. Well-placed objects will also draw attention to a beautiful piece of furniture or architectural feature and make the most of an awkward space by turning it into a point of interest. Nothing, for example, enlivens an empty expanse of wall like a striking composition of prints or paintings.

For collectors, who especially love to live amid their treasures, using favorite objects as accessories is also a particularly effective way to telegraph a passion and project personality into the decor. However, it is not necessary to be a connoisseur to take pleasure in the treasure hunt. Accessories are everywhere at hand: a bronze figurine discovered at a garage sale, a basket picked up at auction, an opalescent shell found on the beach, a pair of candlesticks unpacked from the attic. Even mementos preserved from childhood, such as toys, photographs, or books, can enhance a room's design. Such finishing touches will always succeed because they reflect pride in belongings that not only have particular meaning but were selected for a particular reason as well.

imaginative *details*
in a Bridgehampton farmhouse

SIMPLE OBJECTS IN UNSTUDIED ARRANGEMENTS
bring a sense of time and place — and of whimsy —
to this weekend retreat in Bridgehampton, a seaside
village on the South Fork of Long Island. The
approach is just right for the relaxed mood of a 1730s
farmhouse where rough-hewn beams and plastered
walls are a backdrop for informal furnishings.

Indeed, many accessories have no role in the design
other than to surprise and delight. Rather than
stacks of books, a country pine secretary displays
ranks of mechanical and pull toys, along with
blocks and abacuses, that would have enchanted
children in the late 19th and early 20th centuries.

Decorative accents with a marine theme, including a ship half-model and a bowl full of seaside treasures, perfectly suit this Long Island shore house.

And a living-room corner is brightened by a collection of mercury glass picked up over the years at yard sales, antiques shops, and auctions — simply because it seemed interesting.

Many of the finishing touches make quiet but deliberate references to both the history of the house and the geography of the region. Pewter chargers, tankards, and pots — what would have been the daily dishware for a typical 1700s farm family — for example, are appropriately displayed over the original cooking hearth. At the same time, the wave-worn shells and coral branches and examples of nautical memorabilia splashed around the interiors are refreshing reminders of the nearby beach. ⌐━▷

ABOVE: IN A LIGHTHEARTED GESTURE, CUPBOARD DOORS SWING WIDE TO REVEAL SHELVES OF LATE 19TH- AND EARLY 20TH-CENTURY TOYS.

RIGHT: A TABLETOP SHOWS OFF MERCURY GLASS, A POOR MAN'S ANSWER TO SILVER THAT WAS CRAFTED PRIMARILY IN ENGLAND IN THE 1800S. THE STAGGERED HEIGHTS OF THE VASES AND CANISTERS, WHICH GAINED A DESIRABLE SHEEN FROM THE MERCURY, MAKE A DAZZLING ARRAY.

ABOVE: SOMETHING AS ORDINARY AS DRINKING GLASSES CAN MAKE CLEVER, CASUAL VASES. USING ONE TYPE OF GLASS AND FLOWER CREATES UNITY; PLACEMENT BEFORE A MIRROR DOUBLES THE IMPACT.

BELOW: BEFORE CERAMIC KITCHENWARES BECAME MORE WIDELY AVAILABLE IN THE LATE 1700S, PEWTER WAS USED FOR STORING, PREPARING, AND SERVING FOOD. FLAT PLATES LEANING BEHIND SCULPTURAL VESSELS FORM A LIVELY DISPLAY.

artistic *flourishes*

in a sophisticated apartment

THE OWNERS OF THIS MANHATTAN APARTMENT, designers Richard Mervis and Jeffrey Rosen, not only have an eye for selecting lovely accessories but also possess the talent for arranging them. Encompassing everything from American art pottery to English tea caddies, objects that appeal through their beauty, quirkiness, or history assume their places quietly but purposefully, underscoring the interiors without overwhelming them. "We don't collect to fill space," says Mervis. "One object led to another and became a collection we wanted to display."

Like objects are kept together, which gives the arrangements great impact, and the pieces within each

MINIATURE LOUIS XVI CHAIRS,
FEDERAL TEA CADDIES, AND ART-
GLASS PAPERWEIGHTS BRING A
TOUCH OF URBANE ELEGANCE TO
THIS MANHATTAN LIVING ROOM.

RIGHT: AMONG THE MOST FAMOUS DOG "BREEDS" IS THE STAFFORDSHIRE SPANIEL, PRODUCED IN VARIOUS COLORS AND SIZES BY SEVERAL ENGLISH POTTERIES DURING THE EARLY 19TH CENTURY. USUALLY DESIGNED AND SOLD IN FACING PAIRS, THE SEATED FIGURINES ARE GROUPED HERE IN SETS, WITH SINGLE PIECES WORKED IN TO CREATE A DYNAMIC DISPLAY.

LEFT: COLORED GLASSWARES FROM BOHEMIA, ENGRAVED OR ETCHED TO CREATE A PRETTY INTERPLAY BETWEEN CLEAR AND TINTED SURFACES, HAVE BEEN SOUGHT AFTER BY COLLECTORS SINCE THE 1600S. DECORATED WITH CASTLE AND FOREST SCENES, THESE GLASS BOXES ARE FINE EXAMPLES OF THE ART AND INTRODUCE A BRIGHT BURST OF COLOR INTO THE NEUTRAL PALETTE OF THE LIVING ROOM.

group are carefully composed to evoke a feeling of order. In some instances, a space dictated a certain composition: a broad wall of closet doors, for instance, could accommodate objects only a certain size. The solution was to center two engravings per door, creating a symmetrical display. Other compositions could be more free-flowing. Staffordshire spaniel figurines were shifted around on shelves until a pleasing sense of balance was achieved.

Finding room for objects is seldom a concern for avid collectors focused on the hunt itself, but finding the right spot can be tricky, especially in an interior with strong patterns. A simple striped table skirt proved the perfect backdrop for the busy designs etched into Bohemian ruby-glass boxes, while a large-scale wallpaper pattern gently plays off the shapes of Oriental porcelain. ⌫➤

creative collections
in a Brooklyn brownstone

"MORE IS MORE" IN THIS 19TH-CENTURY ROW house, which seems near bursting with objects that New York designer Fred Cannon could not resist. Items as diverse as medicine bottles, bronze animals, and framed silhouettes distinguish the decor in each of the 10 rooms, some of which are devoted entirely to a single collection. But this idiosyncratic mix of artworks and collectibles works well in the Brooklyn brownstone because it goes hand in hand with the friendly informality of the eclectic antique and contemporary furniture.

Here, displaying varied collections of objects in almost overwhelming numbers calls for a bit of

LEFT: A TIERED ÉTAGÈRE HAS JUST THE RIGHT SCALE FOR EXHIBITING TOY FURNITURE FROM JAPAN TO ADVANTAGE. ITEMS WITH STRONG SHAPES, SUCH AS ENGLISH MEDICINE CONTAINERS, A CALABASH PIPE, AND A MILITARY HAT BOX, BRING INTEREST TO THE ECLECTIC VIGNETTE ON THE TABLE.

BELOW: SMALL SCULPTURES, INCLUDING A BRONZE LION BY THE NOTED 19TH-CENTURY FRENCH SCULPTOR ANTOINE-LOUIS BARYE, CREATE FOCAL POINTS ON LIBRARY SHELVES PACKED WITH BOOKS. THE TABLE SHOWCASES ROCK CRYSTALS AND RUSSIAN LACQUERED BOXES — SOME 40 IN ALL.

OVERLEAF: CUT FROM PAPER, SILHOUETTES WERE AN INEXPENSIVE MEANS OF CAPTURING A LIKENESS IN THE DAYS BEFORE PHOTOGRAPHY; THEY CONTINUE TO APPEAL IN THEIR SIMPLICITY. THE DECOR OF THIS SMALL ROOM GAINS ENORMOUS IMPACT FROM A WALL DISPLAY OF 70 SILHOUETTES MADE IN THE 1700S AND 1800S. ALTHOUGH PIECES HAVE BEEN ADDED OVER TIME, THE ARRANGEMENT HAS BEEN KEPT BALANCED SO AS NOT TO APPEAR CHAOTIC.

flexibility. Select examples of a larger collection, for example, often appear in different rooms as individual accents. With their unusual shapes, 19th-century military hat boxes are striking enough to stand on their own and create interesting vignettes atop library bookcases or bedroom tables. Similarly, a Fo dog figurine or bronze sculpture might sound one striking note on a mantelpiece or shelf.

But the real impact comes when the belongings are grouped en masse — in every available space. Walls are covered with pictures; shelves show off the embossed bindings of leather-bound books; and colorful faux-tiger pillows are piled on sofas. The result? A wonderfully warm feeling of lived-in clutter that truly reflects the passions of the owner. ⌬➤

ABOVE: PUBLISHED IN THE 19TH CENTURY, ENGRAVINGS OF CLASSICAL SCULPTURES IN THE LOUVRE MUSEUM DECORATE THE FOYER AND CONTINUE UP TWO FLIGHTS OF STAIRS.

RIGHT: THE SELECTION OF DECORATIVE ACCESSORIES IN THE PARLOR IS AS ECLECTIC AS THE FURNITURE. TABLETOPS HOLD RUSSIAN ICONS, WHILE A FO DOG GUARDS THE MANTEL AND A REGENCY FAN MADE OF WOOD RESTS ON THE OTTOMAN.

classic *arrangements*

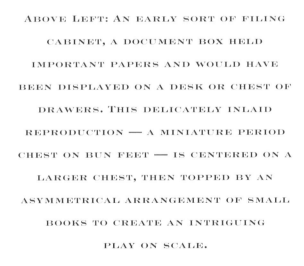

ABOVE LEFT: AN EARLY SORT OF FILING
CABINET, A DOCUMENT BOX HELD
IMPORTANT PAPERS AND WOULD HAVE
BEEN DISPLAYED ON A DESK OR CHEST OF
DRAWERS. THIS DELICATELY INLAID
REPRODUCTION — A MINIATURE PERIOD
CHEST ON BUN FEET — IS CENTERED ON A
LARGER CHEST, THEN TOPPED BY AN
ASYMMETRICAL ARRANGEMENT OF SMALL
BOOKS TO CREATE AN INTRIGUING
PLAY ON SCALE.

LEFT: LARGE, FLAT CUTTING BOARDS
BECOME A BACKDROP FOR SMALLER
BOWLS AND ROLLING PINS IN A HOMEY
PRESENTATION OF WOODENWARE DESIGNED
TO HIGHLIGHT SHAPE AND COLOR.

OPPOSITE: CRYSTAL WAS A LUXURY IN THE EARLY 19TH CENTURY AND WAS PROUDLY DISPLAYED IN THE PARLOR OR DINING ROOM ALONG WITH THE CHINA AND SILVER. PLACED ON TWO LEVELS, EACH OF THESE ENGRAVED GLASSES AND DECANTERS FROM ENGLAND CAN BE CLEARLY SEEN; STACKED CASUALLY, 1830S DISHES IN SHEFFIELD SILVERPLATE KEEP THE ARRANGEMENT FROM LOOKING TOO FORMAL.

BELOW: A TRAY HOLDING CANDLESTICKS AND AN OIL-BURNING LAMP IN AN 18TH-CENTURY HOUSE RECALLS THE CUSTOM OF KEEPING LIGHTING DEVICES BY THE STAIRWELL SO THEY COULD BE CARRIED ALONG TO LIGHT THE WAY TO UPPER FLOORS. THE COMPOSITION IS BEAUTIFUL IN ITS SIMPLICITY.

THE DISPLAY OF HOUSEHOLD OBJECTS HAS ALWAYS played a role in the American interior — even in early Colonial days. To some degree, this was practical: pieces like candlesticks and dishes that were in frequent use, for example, needed to be kept conveniently at hand.

However, possessions were also put on show for the sheer enjoyment that being surrounded by beauty brings. And thanks to a universal instinct to make the utilitarian beautiful, even the most mundane necessities could be attractive enough to a make a contribution. An everyday tin lantern might be pierced, for example — not only to let the light shine through but to create pattern. And even as early as the 1600s, carving and painting embellished the simple wooden plates, bowls, and utensils that preceded pewter and ceramic wares in the Colonies. China, silver, and crystal were also available to families of means, and some furniture was ready-made for showing off household finery. The dish dressers and corner cupboards, or "boffets," of the 1700s, as well as the sideboards of the 1800s, provided surfaces ideal for display.

In truth, however, it is not so much *where* objects are shown off as *how* that is important. Even something as apparently unstudied as a stack of beautifully bound old books can lend a subtle but tasteful touch to a room. Indeed, while individual accessories can be admired of themselves, they become even more compelling when grouped. A good, classic arrangement will highlight their forms and decoration while providing an interesting overall composition that considers color and material, achieves a certain balance, and takes advantage of lighting to become a focal point within the larger space. ⬳

RIGHT: GLAZED-FRONT CABINETS WERE FIRST POPULAR IN THE 1700S, WHEN GLASS BECAME MORE AFFORDABLE AND THE WEALTHY HAD ORIENTAL PORCELAINS AND OTHER LUXURY ITEMS TO SHOWCASE. LIKE MANY SUCH PIECES, THIS VITRINE OF THE PERIOD FEATURES SCALLOPED SHELVES DESIGNED FOR HOLDING PLATES; ADDITIONAL BOTTLES, BOOKS, AND BOTANICAL PRINTS ARE MIXED IN FOR A MORE CASUAL ARRANGEMENT.

BELOW: BANDBOXES, THE CARDBOARD CONTAINERS FOR HATS, RIBBONS, AND TRINKETS SO FASHIONABLE IN THE EARLY 1800S, WERE PROUDLY PUT ON DISPLAY BY YOUNG LADIES LUCKY ENOUGH TO OWN THEM. WITH THEIR BRIGHT WALLPAPER COVERINGS, THEY REMAIN POPULAR TODAY FOR STACKING IN COLORFUL DISPLAYS.

ABOVE: A SAMOVAR AND SCULPTURES IN
SILVER JOIN CRYSTAL CANDLESTICKS WITH
CUT PENDANTS FOR AN ELEGANT VIGNETTE
SUITED TO A FORMAL DINING ROOM.

ABOVE RIGHT: TIN LANTERNS HANGING
FROM A PRIMITIVE PEG RACK PROVIDE
PERIOD TOUCHES IN THE PANTRY OF AN
18TH-CENTURY FARMHOUSE.

RIGHT: AN ARRAY OF WATCH STANDS —
IN WHICH GENTLEMEN OF THE 18TH AND
19TH CENTURIES STORED THEIR POCKET
WATCHES AT NIGHT, THEREBY DEVISING
A BEDSIDE CLOCK — LINE UP
IN A WHIMSICAL PARADE ATOP A DESK
FROM THE HUDSON RIVER VALLEY.

Elements of *design*
picture *displays*

ABOVE LEFT: A CAREFULLY BUT CASUALLY
COMPOSED GROUP OF SELF-SUPPORTING
PICTURE FRAMES — IN VARIOUS SHAPES,
SIZES, AND MATERIALS — ADDS INTEREST
AND DIMENSION TO A DRESSER TOP.

ABOVE: IN A TIGHT, BALANCED GROUPING,
ENGRAVED PERIOD PORTRAITS OF ENGLISH
NOBLES CREATE A FOCAL POINT ON A
LARGE EXPANSE OF WALL WHILE QUIETLY
UNDERSCORING THE FORMALITY OF AN
18TH-CENTURY VIRGINIA BEDCHAMBER.

LEFT: A DEEP MOLDING PROVIDES A STAGE
FOR PAINTINGS. THOUGH PART OF A
PLANNED SYMMETRICAL DISPLAY,
THE ARTWORKS LEANING AGAINST THE
WALL BRING A SPONTANEOUS LOOK
TO THE VIGNETTE.

BELOW: PORTRAITURE WAS THE MOST PRESTIGIOUS TYPE OF PAINTING IN THE 18TH CENTURY, AND PICTURES WERE DISPLAYED PROMINENTLY IN RECEPTION ROOMS. THE PORTRAITS IN THE GREAT HALL OF THIS 1785 HOUSE FORM A CLASSIC "TRIANGLE" AROUND THE FIREPLACE, WHERE THEY ARE SURE TO BE NOTICED.

BELOW RIGHT: SLIPPING PHOTOS INTO A MIRROR FRAME IS ONE WAY TO ACCESSORIZE A ROOM WHILE ADDING AN INFORMAL, LIVED-IN TOUCH. THE LATE 19TH-CENTURY MILK-GLASS HOLDER ON THE MANTEL WAS SPECIFICALLY DESIGNED FOR PHOTOGRAPHS, WHICH WERE ALL THE RAGE IN THE VICTORIAN ERA.

DECORATING THE WALLS WITH ARTWORK WAS A rare practice in early Colonial times; only the very wealthy could afford to sit for portraits and usually had to travel to England to have a likeness rendered. Before the end of the 17th century, paintings of any kind appeared only in the best homes of New England and the South.

With increasing prosperity in the 1700s, however, it was possible to imitate the Continental fashion for hanging paintings, prints, and maps in the common rooms, often high up on the wall. Portraits, by then more available from American artists, remained the most prestigious art form into the Federal era, but landscapes and seascapes also became popular. Framed simply in gilt or black ovals or rectangles, such works were still mounted high, though they might be suspended from brass rings or ornamental cords rather than hung "blind."

By the early decades of the 1800s, pictures had become so common that it was necessary to pay more attention to their arrangement. While a large painting might occupy a wall by itself, smaller works were placed in balanced groups, including symmetrical pairs. Householders were just then discovering what is now taken for granted: not only are pictures beautiful in themselves, but their display works as an effective decorative element as well. ◄

Elements of design
fireplaces & mantels

ABOVE LEFT: FIREPLACE SURROUNDS
CONFORM TO PERIOD STYLE JUST AS
FURNITURE DOES. THIS EXAMPLE, BUILT IN
1766, WAS REMODELED IN THE EARLY 1800S
TO REFLECT THE FEDERAL STYLE. TYPICAL
NEOCLASSICAL TOUCHES INCLUDE REEDED
PILASTERS, FLUTED MOLDING, AND THREE
PATERAE, OR ELLIPTICAL ORNAMENTS.
CANDLESTICKS AND PORCELAINS WERE
COMMON ACCESSORIES OF THE PERIOD.

LEFT: AS REFLECTED BY THIS REPRODUCTION
FIREPLACE DESIGN, A MORE ORNATE
TREATMENT WITH DEEP DENTIL MOLDING,
MARBLE SURROUND, AND A PANELED
OVERMANTEL WITH "EARS" WAS IN FAVOR IN
THE MID-18TH CENTURY.
A FIVE-PIECE DELFTWARE GARNITURE
ACCENTS THE FORMAL STYLE.

OPPOSITE: FIREBOARDS WERE IN FASHION IN THE EARLY 1800S, PRIMARILY TO CONCEAL AN UNUSED FIREPLACE BUT ALSO TO PREVENT SOOT AND BIRDS FROM ENTERING THE HOUSE. WHILE SOME WERE PAINTED WITH TROMPE-L'OEIL FIREPLACE INTERIORS, LANDSCAPE SCENES SUCH AS THIS WERE ALSO POPULAR. A LINEUP OF CLOCKS, PICTURES, AND LAMPS ON THE MANTEL COMPLETES THE FIREPLACE DECORATION.

BELOW: PIECES OF POTTERY IN STAGGERED SIZES ARE SILHOUETTED AGAINST A PLAIN-PAINTED OVERMANTEL. THE CENTRAL PANEL, FRAMED BY MOLDING, WAS MEANT TO RECEIVE A PAINTING.

A SOURCE OF LIGHT AND HEAT, A PLACE FOR cooking, and a conveyor of comfort, the fireplace was among the most important structural elements in the Colonial interior — and was generally the largest as well. Little wonder that attention was lavished on turning this dominant feature into an attractive focal point. Although a functional cooking hearth might have nothing more than a rough-hewn log mantel, fireplaces in the formal parlor or a house's other "public" rooms were treated with more gracious designs as early as the 1680s. At that time it became fashionable among the well-to-do to frame the opening with molding, add a shallow shelf, or incorporate a mantel into the wall paneling. In the 18th century, the complete, integrated surround developed. Supported on brackets or pilasters and decorated with carvings and moldings, the mantel shelf became more prominent; marble or tiles might face the opening; and a cupboard or panel meant to accommodate a painting surmounted the whole.

By the late 1700s, the fireplace had become such a fashion target that accessories were designed especially for it. One traditional accessory was the fireboard, which was used to cover the black hole of the opening in warm weather and was typically painted or covered with a patterned wallpaper. In addition to displaying clocks, candlesticks, and other domestic wares, householders could also decorate with a stylish fireplace garniture, a set of porcelain jars and vases (usually five) designed specifically for the mantelpiece.

The mantel, of course, remains the ideal spot for arrangements of pottery, candlesticks, pictures, flowers, and favorite collectibles. Shown off on this ready-made display area, groupings of virtually any object can have as much impact as a painting or other work of art. ❧

flowers & plants

ABOVE LEFT: THE LARGE, VOLUPTUOUS
BLOOMS OF OLD-FASHIONED ROSES ARE
CLASSIC; THEY NEED NEITHER A SPECIAL
CONTAINER NOR ARRANGEMENT.

ABOVE: USING DRIED PLANTS IS AN IDEAL
WAY TO ENJOY NATURAL DECORATION
DURING THE DORMANT GROWING SEASON.
BRANCHES OF BITTERSWEET CASCADE FROM
AN URN ON THIS BACK STAIRWELL.

LEFT: MATCHING IVY TOPIARIES, COMBINED
WITH CLASSICAL URNS AND A LATE 18TH-
CENTURY MIRROR, ARE APPROPRIATELY
FORMAL ACCENTS IN THIS FEDERAL-
STYLE LIVING ROOM.

LITTLE IS KNOWN ABOUT HOW COLONISTS USED flowers and plants indoors before the 1800s. Certainly there was a fascination with New World specimens, and ornamental plants were sometimes grown along with medicinal and edible varieties in home gardens. Decorating with flowers and greens was an established custom in Europe — especially in Holland — and settlers may well have followed that fashion, if only on special occasions. At the very least, plants did come inside for practical reasons. For example, herbs — used for cooking and dye making — were hung to dry from rafters and racks. By the early 1800s, however, Americans were using plants more frequently for decoration, whether as cut flowers in a vase or as potted greens, which were thought to freshen the dry air produced by coal-burning stoves. The importation of vases, flower bricks, and bulb pots from Asia and Europe also suggests that plants were becoming an important element in a room's design.

Plants and flowers are still a pleasure and are extremely effective finishing touches. A trim topiary might accent a formal look, for example, while dried flowers and berries evoke the natural feeling of country style. Potted plants mix well with decorative objects to create interesting groupings — and nothing can compete with a bouquet of fresh flowers to tantalize the senses. ◂

ABOVE LEFT: BEARING A PROMISE OF SPRING, FORCED BULBS BRING COLOR INDOORS AHEAD OF NATURE'S SCHEDULE. NARCISSUS, ABLOOM IN LATE WINTER, GROW IN WOODEN CONTAINERS THAT BLEND WITH THE RUSTIC FLAVOR OF A CABIN.

LEFT: DRIED BUNCHES OF VIBURNUM BLOOMS MIX WITH EVERGREEN SPRIGS, ORNAMENTAL SEED PODS, AND CITRUS FRUITS IN A LUSH BOUQUET.

INDEX

CREDITS

Photographers

Mary Ellen Bartley: page 99 (top right and bottom left).

Gordon Beall: pages 7 (top right), 40 (top and bottom), 41, 42, 43, 120 (bottom), 121, 129 (bottom), 160, 165, and 182 (top).

Craig Becker: pages 86 (top left, top right, and bottom), 94 (top right), and 162 (bottom).

Robert Benson: pages 112, 112-113, 114, 115 (top and bottom), and 122 (bottom).

Ron Blunt: pages 119 and 184 (top right).

Joe Bowman: page 189 (top).

Jim Cooper: spine (bottom); pages 13 (bottom right), 28 (top and bottom), 29, 30 (top, bottom left, and bottom right), 31, 32, 33 (top and bottom), 78, 78-79, 80, 81, 82 (top left and bottom), 88 (top), 99 (top left), 122 (top), 123 (top right and bottom), 135 (bottom left), 176, 176-177, 178 (top and bottom), and 179 (top and bottom).

Richard Felber: page 13 (top right).

Tria Giovan: pages 4-5, 66, 66-67, 68, 69, 90 (right), 92 (bottom), 126 (top left), 135 (bottom right), 152 (bottom left), 153, 154, 156 (top left), 168, 168-169, 170, 170-171, 171 (top and bottom), 180 (top right), 185 (right), and 188 (top left).

Gross & Daley: pages 14 (top and bottom), 15, 16, 17 (top and bottom), 18, 19 (top left, top right, and bottom), and 183 (top right).

Kari Haavisto: pages 6 (top), 11, and 83 (right).

Mick Hales: front cover; pages 20, 21, 22, 23, 24-25, 26, 27 (top and bottom), 172, 172-173, 174 (top and bottom), 175 (top and bottom), 184 (bottom), and 186 (top right).

John Hall: pages 84-85, 91, 104, 104-105, 106 (top and bottom), 107, 116 (top right), 130, 183 (top left), 185 (left), and 188 (bottom).

Francis Hammond: pages 34, 35, 36 (top and bottom), 37, 38, and 38-39.

Erik Kvalsvik: back cover (top right), front flap; pages 6 (bottom), 7 (bottom), 8, 9 (top left), 12, 44, 45 (top and bottom), 46 (top and bottom), 47, 48, 49, 50-51, 59, 60, 61 (top left, top right, and bottom right), 82 (top right), 83 (left), 87, 88 (bottom), 88-89, 92 (top right), 94 (top left), 98, 116 (top left), 117, 120 (top left, top right), 124 (bottom), 128 (top left), 129 (top), 133, 134, 144, 144-145, 146 (top and bottom), 147, 148, 148-149, 150, 151, 155 (top and bottom), 156 (bottom), 157 (right), 162 (top right), 167 (top right, bottom right, and bottom left), 180 (top left), 181, 183 (bottom), 186 (bottom), and 187.

Peter Margonelli: pages 9 (top right), 61 (bottom left), 100, 100-101, 102, 103, 124 (top right), 166, 167 (top left), and 186 (top left).

Maura McEvoy: pages 2, 9 (bottom left), 123 (top left), 125, 135 (top left and top right), 140, 140-141, 142 (top and bottom), 143 (top and bottom), 158 (top right), 162 (top left), and 163.

Jeff McNamara: pages 62, 62-63, 64, 65 (top and bottom), 65 (bottom), 93, 116 (bottom), 118-119, 128 (top right), 131 (bottom), 157 (left), 158 (bottom), and 180 (bottom).

Michael Mundy: back cover (top left and bottom left); pages 9 (bottom right), 13 (bottom left), 74, 74-75, 76, 77, 92 (top left), 95, 99 (bottom right), 108, 108-109, 110-111, 111, 124 (top left), 126 (bottom), 159, 160-161, 182 (bottom), and 189 (bottom).

Cheryl Pendleton: pages 13 (top left), 127, and 128 (bottom).

Scalamandré: pages 7 (top left) and 97.

Mark Schreyer: page 90 (left).

Alan Shortall: page 152 (top and bottom right).

Al Teufen: page 156 (top right).

John Vaughan: page 158 (top left).

Judith Watts: spine (top), back cover (bottom right); pages 52 (top and bottom), 53, 54, 55 (top and bottom), 56 (top and bottom), 57, 70, 70-71, 72 (top and bottom), 73, 94 (bottom), 126 (top right), 136, 136-137, 138 (top and bottom), 139 (top and bottom), and 184 (top left).

Tom Yee: pages 131 (top) and 188 (top right).

Designers

Cozy Pelzer: pages 20-27.
Dan Carithers: pages 28-33.
James Dean: pages 40-43.
Clare Fraser: pages 52-57.
Matt Larkin: pages 70-73.
Charlotte Moss: pages 74-77.
Holly Holden: pages 104-107.
Beth Copeland Williams: pages 108-111.
Eric Cohler: pages 136-139.
Richard Mervis and Jeffrey Rosen: pages 172-175.
Fred Cannon: pages 176-179.